Advance Praise for

People Tools for Love and Relationships

"This book is for anyone who is in love or would like to be. I know Alan's advice will help you deepen your relationships."

—Steve Harvey

Host of the Steve Harvey Show
Author of *Act Like a Success, Think Like a Success*

"Alan is an adept and experienced guide on the journey from 'me' to 'us.'"

—John Gray

Best-selling author of *Men Are from Mars, Women Are from Venus*

"The best teachings are always simple and wise. Alan offers excellent wisdom with heartfelt stories, practical tools, and an invitation to remember what matters most. We need this in relationships more than anything."

—Jack Kornfield

Author of *A Path with Heart*

"*People Tools for Love and Relationships* is gentle and wise guidance into the wisdom of how to look for, find, and keep love . . . what could be more precious?"

—Frederic Luskin, PhD

Author of *Forgive for Good* and
Director of the Stanford Forgiveness Project

rh

"We think love is all about connection but having the right relationship skills is just as important. Unfortunately, we're not taught them at school and that's why Alan Fox's work is so important."

—Andrew G. Marshall

Marital therapist and author of *Wake Up and Change Your Life: How to Survive a Crisis and Be Stronger, Wiser and Happier*

"With truly useable ideas, Alan Fox forces a keen look at the simplicity behind healthy, lasting loving relationships."

—Liz Pryor

Author of *What Did I Do Wrong?*

"Where there's a will there's a way is actually backwards. In reality, where there's a way, people find the will to do whatever it takes to become fulfilled, satisfied and love happily ever after. *People Tools for Love and Relationships* is *that* way and *your* way."

—Mark Goulston, MD

Author of *Just Listen: Discover the Secret to Getting Through to Absolutely Anyone*

"If you want to improve your connections to others—and we all do—this book is for you. Alan's wisdom and humor is engaging and helpful. He will remind you that we all have the ability to enhance our relationships."

—Michelle Skeen

Psychologist and author of *Love Me, Don't Leave Me*

"Alan Fox demonstrates yet again the depth of his heart and the power of his mind to guide us into a better perspective. Each one of his books has the appearance of an easy read, and they are. However, as the content floats into your head you suddenly find yourself working to use his wisdom in your own circumstances. Alan's words penetrate and influence in positive and healthy ways! I love this most recent book and look forward to what he will be doing next. What a treasure!"

—**Dr. Deb Carlin**
Author of *Build the Strength Within*

"*People Tools for Love and Relationships* is filled with wisdom nuggets about love and relationships gleaned from the trenches of life by a person who clearly is the embodiment of the singular message that how we handle all our relationships is the key to happiness. That's it!! And he illustrates it with accessible and compelling stories. Everyone should read this recipe for life."

—**Harville Hendrix, PhD** and **Helen LaKelly Hunt, PhD**
Co-authors of *Making Marriage Simple*

"Wise and funny, relationship guru Alan Fox shows you how to add more love and passion to your life. This is a valuable guide to building deeper, more meaningful connections with others."

—**Katherine Woodward Thomas**
Author of *Calling in "The One"*

"When it comes to loving relationships, sometimes we just need a bright idea or two to jolt us out of boring or unhealthy patterns. In *People Tools for Love and Relationships*, Alan Fox offers just that: a toolkit for finding and keeping love that a reader can begin to use immediately. Told in short, highly readable lessons, Fox relies on his own relationship experience and that of others to offer advice that is wise, witty, poignant, and always useful. A book for everyone, from people looking for love to those striving to keep the spark alive after decades together."

—**Karl Pillemer, PhD**

Author of 30 *Lessons for Loving:*
Advice from the Wisest Americans on Love, Relationships, and Marriage

Praise for

People Tools for Business: 50 Strategies for Building Success, Creating Wealth, and Finding Happiness

"We all want to be happy and successful at work and in our lives . . . Alan Fox shares invaluable insights that can help you make a career out of being happy."

—Tony Hsieh

CEO of Zappos.com, Inc. and author of *Delivering Happiness*

"With refreshing candor, Alan Fox shares the invaluable lessons that he has garnered over an extremely successful, forty-five-year career."

—Brent Kessel

CEO, Abacus Wealth Partners and author of *It's Not About the Money*

"Wise and playful. These charmingly straightforward and practical tools will assist you and add joy to your business life."

—Jack Kornfield

Psychologist, author, and founder of Spirit Rock Meditation Center

"Read this book—it's like having a long, satisfying conversation with your own professional mentor (and mine), Alan Fox."

—Jill E. Fox

From the foreword to *People Tools for Business*

Fox is a die-hard optimist, and his enthusiasm, good humor, and belief that all situations can improve for the better carries over into this sequel to the best-selling *People Tools*. Designed to appeal to people at all levels of business, from student to manager to retiree, this guide to constant self-improvement urges readers up the "glass staircase." A play on the "glass ceiling," this phrase refers to steps which any person can take to reach the top. The five stairs are Confidence, Home, Education, Assertiveness, and Passion—CHEAP.

The book's concept is a toolbox, comprising 50 "people tools" that will help readers achieve more in business and life. Illustrating his points with entertaining stories from his own life, Fox encourages readers to adopt tools such as "advertise your mistakes," "don't run out of cash," "be a contrarian," don't try to be right all the time, and focus on the future.

The tone is homey but not condescending, and the mix of practical, emotional and behavioral tools make this a guide likely to inspire across the board. "You are the sole proprietor of your own life," proclaims Fox—and it's hard to imagine the reader who wouldn't respond to this upbeat message.

—*Publishers Weekly*
(review posted 9.8.14)

Praise for Alan C. Fox's *New York Times* Best Seller
*People Tools: 54 Strategies for Building Relationships,
Creating Joy, and Embracing Prosperity*

"Alan Fox has great tools for emotional intelligence, wisdom, clarity and directness. Develop and use them to live well, and your life will grow better for it."

—Jack Kornfield

Psychologist, author, and founder of Spirit Rock Meditation Center

"*People Tools* is a gem of down-to-earth, practical advice on wise living. In simple, straightforward prose, Alan Fox illuminates insights that are often in plain sight but frequently overlooked. A very helpful book."

—Joseph Goldstein

Author and co-founder of Insight Meditation Center

"Reading *People Tools* is like having a wise, loving and funny friend take you by the hand, and gently but surely lead you to a better place. Everyone could benefit from reading it."

—Sharon Salzberg

Author of *Lovingkindness* and *Real Happiness*

People
Tools
for Love and
Relationships

Other Books in the
People Tools Series by Alan C. Fox

People Tools:
54 Strategies for Building Relationships,
Creating Joy, and Embracing Prosperity
(2014)

People Tools for Business:
50 Strategies for Building Success,
Creating Wealth, and Finding Happiness
(2014)

People Tools

Tools

for Love and Relationships

The Journey from Me to Us

ALAN C. FOX

SelectBooks, Inc.
New York

People Tools™ is a trademark of People Tools 13 LLC.

This edition published by SelectBooks, Inc.
For information address SelectBooks, Inc., New York, New York.

First Edition

ISBN 978-1-59079-356-5

Library of Congress Cataloging-in-Publication Data
Fox, Alan C.
People tools for love and relationships : the journey from me to us / Alan C. Fox. -- First Edition.
pages cm
ISBN 978-1-59079-356-5 (pbk. : alk. paper) 1. Interpersonal relations.
2. Love. I. Title.
HM1106.F694 2015
302--dc23
2015008423

Book design by Janice Benight

Manufactured in the United States of America
10 9 8 7 6 5 4 3 2 1

This book is dedicated to all those who have been, and will be, themselves dedicated to bringing to you the concept that you *do* make a difference in the lives of others, and that with time you can make a significant positive transformation in your own life.

I especially thank my friend and editor Nancy Miller, my daughter Sara for dedicating herself to writing the foreword, and my wife Daveen, who has waited up nights and saved both you and me from many "glitches."

I want to give thanks to Lauren Hunsaker, Kat Corona Pilgrim, Joel Pitney, and Asha Blake, who have contributed so much of their time and enthusiasm; to my cover designer Chin-Yee Lai; to Jane Wesman and Felicia Sinusas, who have generated a great deal of publicity for the *People Tools* series; to Kenzi and Kenichi Sugihara at SelectBooks and to Chris Bell at Midpoint Trade Books; and to Nancy Sugihara and Jeffrey Gerretse, who have helped to make my words accurate and presentable on the page.

This book is primarily dedicated to you, my reader, who is the "sine qua non" ("without this, nothing") of the considerable efforts put forth by everyone above. You are the only one who can truly bring *People Tools* to life in the world.

CONTENTS

By Sara Fox, B.S., M.S., MBA

When I was growing up we never had fewer than ten people living in our house. Siblings, cousins, and family friends filled the bedrooms and overflowed into the common areas. By the time my youngest sister was born the only space available for her was a small alcove that we converted into a glorified closet. Space was tight at the Fox home, but all were welcome.

This type of magnanimity and inclusivity is typical of my parents. Blessed with prosperity, Alan and Daveen are happiest when sharing what they have with others. Though they certainly enjoy the camaraderie of a bustling household, their primary intention for opening their home has always been to enable people who might otherwise lack the support system to pursue their dreams and ambitions. This propensity is encapsulated beautifully by the South African term *ubuntu*, which refers to the interconnectedness of all of life and the responsibility inherent in our connection.

Dad's adage has always been "If you can only have one skill in life, getting along with others is the one to have." I wholeheartedly agree. Humans need (and want!) to connect. Connection gives purpose and meaning to our lives—it's why we're here. Spectacular, yet simultaneously terrifying, most of us struggle in this essential human endeavor.

Excited as I was to make new friends the morning of my first day of school, I was unsure how to go about it and afraid of what others would think of me. So there I stood on the playground, motionless and alone, when another little girl approached me. "Hi. I like your pigtails," she said. "Thanks," I replied, and quickly said, "I like your dress. Do you want to play on the swings with me?" "Yeah!" she exclaimed and off we ran. By being comfortable herself, she gave me permission to be the same. For the next twelve years the two of us were practically inseparable.

While most relationships are not this straightforward, this experience illustrates an important point: When it comes to cultivating a relationship, intention can only take you so far—specifically, to the edge of your comfort zone. This is the point of entry where real connection can be made as well as the place most of us get stuck.

That's why my father has written this book comprised of knowledge, insight, and wisdom gathered over almost thirty-five years of marriage and fifty years in business—to empower you with the tools needed to more comfortably and effectively navigate the journey from me to us. Use of these tools will help you cultivate ease in your relationships and in your life by transforming what were once problems into incredible opportunities for growth and connection.

Take, for example, my graduate school roommate, Becca. An energetic, smart, and generous woman, Becca was strong and capable, but strove to please everyone and struggled to say no. Afraid to disappoint anyone, Becca had a hard time setting boundaries and was constantly doing things for others.

One afternoon she collapsed on the sofa, exhausted and overwhelmed. I shared with her what I had learned about the necessity of taking care of myself before others (Tool 15: Put on Your Own Oxygen Mask First) and reminded her that real connection is only possible when we are honest with others (Tool 9: Truth Is the Long Cut). It was as though a tremendous weight had been lifted from her shoulders. With courage and practice, Becca was finally able to let go of who she thought she should be and embrace who she really was (Tool 4: How to Be the Right Person).

Connection is an art, but it's also a science. For as long as I can remember, my mom has told me that my lesson in life is patience. While I find the opportunity to practice this skill in many aspects of my life (driving, anyone?), I've learned that patience is particularly important in the midst of an argument or misunderstanding.

A few years ago my boyfriend, who hadn't been answering his phone, arrived home over two hours late. "Where have you been?" I demanded as soon as he walked in the door. It turns out he had been visiting his cousin with leukemia and had accidentally left his phone at the hospital. He felt sad and tender and needed compassion—not criticism—when he saw me.

Remembering this experience is a good reminder that just because it may feel to me like it's the right time to discuss something, this doesn't mean it *is* the right time (Tool 29: Timing). By focusing exclusively on the goal we wish to attain, we miss out on imperative information revealed in the process (Tool 27: The Field of Battle).

For years in yoga I tried doing a handstand only to be met with frustration and injury. It was only once I let go of my desired outcome (doing a handstand) and focused on the process needed to achieve it (developing core strength, balance, shoulder stability, etc.) that I made progress. The same is true in relationships—to make a connection with someone we must focus more on the process than the outcome (Tool 42: Belt Buckle, Revisited).

The tools offered here have fundamentally expanded my perception and changed the way that I live and love. I know it can seem overwhelming—especially if, like me, you're a perfectionist who prefers to do something perfectly or not at all. But the truth is there's no such thing as perfect. An all-or-nothing mentality will only create anxiety and leave you paralyzed.

By embracing your imperfection, you honor yourself as well as your relationships (Tool 48: Make the Most of Today). Also, remember that to do anything well it takes practice. Aristotle said, "We are what we repeatedly do. Excellence, then, is not an act but a habit." Professional athletes spend countless hours practicing their skills in order to make it appear effortless on game day (Tool 3: Finding a Relationship—Be Prepared).

The tools in this book are practical and easy to implement. They may change your life, but only if you practice. Start by picking a few of the tools that really resonate with you, and begin practicing them with the people in your life. By experimenting with even small changes in our lives, especially in our relationships, we can alter the course of our path and open ourselves up to tremendous growth and positive change. May this book help to imbue you with the tools to build lasting, loving relationships with yourself and the important beings in your life.

INTRODUCTION

In December of 2008 my family and I traveled to Antarctica. During our two-week journey I read the book *Endurance: Shackleton's Incredible Voyage* by Alfred Lansing.

On November 21, 1915, one of Shackleton's two ships, the *Endurance*, was crushed and sank beneath the Antarctic ice. When Shackleton gave the order to abandon the ship, he and his crew of twenty-eight men and seventy dogs camped on the sea ice for two months until the ice melted and they could launch their lifeboats. They spent more than a year struggling to survive while making their way back to civilization.

Near the end of this ordeal, Shackleton chose a small party to undertake a harrowing thirty-two-mile land crossing of an island in the Falkland Islands to reach a populated whaling station that would be their salvation.

When traversing the mountainous terrain, he and his two companions found themselves stranded in snow during the dimming light of late afternoon at an estimated altitude of almost a mile. The nighttime temperature could easily drop below zero and a blizzard was possible. They had little food. Their clothing was tattered and threadbare, and their useful supplies were down to an adze and fifty feet of rope.

They would not survive the hours-long trek in darkness down the mountain to the whaling station.

Shackleton devised a plan.

"Let's coil the rope underneath us, hold onto each other, and slide right down the mountain."

One of his men objected, saying, "That's crazy. We're certain to hit a rock, or fall off a cliff and die."

Shackleton replied, "We are certain to die if we remain here, and we're certain to freeze if we continue to hike down. Our only salvation is to slide."

A few hours later the three starving shipmates staggered into Stromness Whaling Station. They arrived at the house of Thøralf Sørlle, the factory manager who had previously met Shackleton. Upon opening the front door of his home Sørlle failed to recognize the emaciated men.

Shackleton immediately set to work to organize the rescue of his other crewmembers.

*   *   *

Each of us, at some point in our lives, has felt forsaken, as if we were stranded and freezing in the snow, facing severe danger or death. At that moment we can choose to stay stuck, allow fear to harden our hearts, and hope that a miracle will save us. Or we can emulate Shackleton, take charge of our lives and find our way to safety. We can seize the opportunity to slide down an uncertain slope to save ourselves and our partners.

We each must recognize that the partnership of "us" is accompanied by risk. Each of our journeys of deep friendship and love has the potential to end in loss. But I have found no better alternative than to fully explore the world, and my life, with a partner. I prefer to live not only as "me" but also to enthusiastically embark upon the exhilarating and exhausting adventure of a lifetime, the journey from "me" to "us."

People
Tools
for Love and
Relationships

THE KEY IS YOU

Every human being on Earth, including you, is like a house with windows that look out upon the world. Each person, each metaphorical house, is surrounded by a fence, and that fence has a sign on it which says "No Trespassing." And each individual, each house, has a front door, and that door has a lock. To pass through the door, to enter the house, to have a relationship, you must possess the key.

When I was ten years old I told my mother that I wanted to invite only girls to my birthday party. My mother said, "No. You can't just invite girls. You have to invite at least one boy."

"But Mom, boys are so silly."

"Alan, you have to invite at least one boy."

So I did. I invited ten girls and one boy to my party, and that celebration may have been the best birthday party of my life. I've always enjoyed the company of women.

A few years later I realized that I wanted a girl to love me. I didn't really know what love was, but I knew it would be wonderful, and I wanted it. How could I get a girl to love me?

Who could I ask about it? No one. I certainly couldn't talk to my parents. They would be embarrassed and probably say something easy and unhelpful like, "You're too young. You'll find out when you're older."

I wasn't about to ask my younger brother. What does a younger brother know? Nothing. And he might tattle to Mom. Other boys were useless to me, not capable of, or interested in, any serious conversation.

And I absolutely, positively, wasn't going to ask a girl. That would be far too embarrassing. I couldn't. For many years I just couldn't. So, I had to figure out what to do all by myself.

I decided to do some research.

I haunted the local library. I read every magazine that I thought might help, but still didn't find my answer.

Then I learned from a friendly librarian how to use the card catalogue, and I found books that I thought might contain the solution. I carried home ten books at a time because that was the maximum the library would allow me to check out.

"What are you reading, Alan?" my mother would ask.

"Oh, nothing, Mom."

She must have wondered, because week after week I checked out ten books and ploughed through every one of them—psychology books, romance novels, philosophical works—everything I could find that I thought might be helpful. I was a pretty fast reader, and I spent months searching for my answer. But I discovered nothing.

Then, one day, I found it. I finally came across one sentence buried deep in a single book that simply said, "To have someone love you, love them first." At last I had discovered the answer I was looking for.

And though I certainly didn't know it at the time, that sentence is probably the best single bit of relationship advice I have ever read.

I'll say it again so that you will remember it, and will be encouraged to release the love, which might otherwise remain imprisoned inside of you.

"To have someone love you, love them first."

We always begin a relationship as strangers. You are locked in your house, I in mine. We might live next to each other, or across the street or halfway around the world from each other. But we always begin as strangers, even if we meet for the first time when we are five years old.

The key to my persuading you to open that gate in the fence in front of your house is me. The key to my getting you to unbolt your front door is me. No one else can be my stand-in to meet you and become your friend.

Let's jump ahead a little. You have found the way to open someone else's gate, have walked through their yard, and found the front door unlocked. In short, you now have a relationship. Good work. Remember that the key to this beginning was you. And once you've established a relationship, how do you maintain and improve it?

Again, the answer remains—it is you.

My first wife and I had dated for five years before we married, and then we were married for seven years before the "happily ever after" began to fade. In my second marriage I woke up from the dream of a wonderful marriage after seven days. Each time I was certain that the problem was . . . can you guess? Of course. The problem each time was my wife. If one or the other would have changed I could have lived happily with her until today. But each of them failed me. They were inadequate.

Or did I fail them? Could *I*, possibly, have been inadequate *myself*?

Or did we fail each other? Did we lack something? Were we deficient in the knowledge, experience, or the will to work out our differences?

I still remember two sessions with a therapist in which my first wife, Jo Anne, said to him, "This is what I want Alan to change about himself."

The therapist turned to me. "Alan, what do you have to say about that?"

I was shocked. It was Jo Anne who had to change. "I won't change that," I said.

"Jo Anne?"

"Make him change."

"Alan?"

"I won't change that." And so it went. Neither of us budged.

So after ten years of marriage and with three young children, we separated, and then we divorced. Neither of us was willing to change. Nor were we willing to live with each other as we were.

Conventional wisdom today tells us that both people in a relationship are responsible for its success, and that we must work together to get through the rough patches. That may be true, but all too often each party ends up saying out loud or thinking, "I have done my part. I have changed. The remaining problem is him (or her)."

That way of thinking can easily turn into an endless loop of finger-pointing and self- righteousness, and that is exactly where the partners in the relationship often remain trapped. If you need his or her cooperation you are absolutely stuck if "the light bulb doesn't want to change."

I have good news. I have finally discovered that there is only one solution that will work, and that is to take full responsibility myself for creating and maintaining my ideal relationship. I'm not going to blame my parents, my wife, or the stars. I'm not going to blame anyone. I'm going to do my level best to make every relationship I have work, and work well. By taking that approach, my relationships have a chance—a good chance. To put it another way, the key to a great relationship is simply *you*.

This is, perhaps, the most important relationship secret that you will ever need to remember. It is the theme of this book, and deserves its own paragraph:

The key to any successful relationship is you.

PEOPLE TOOL
FOR LOVE & RELATIONSHIPS
2

ATTENTION MUST BE PAID

The worst sin toward our fellow creatures is not to hate them,
but to be indifferent to them: that's the essence of inhumanity.

—GEORGE BERNARD SHAW
The Devil's Disciple

There are two ways of spreading light: to be
The candle or the mirror that reflects it.

—EDITH WHARTON
Vesalius in Zante

The desire for attention is deeply human. At work and at home, in our relationships we want to feel special and that others are paying attention to us. This is why I go out of my way to make sure that I give my full attention to whomever I'm with during the time that I'm with them.

But my philosophy can sometimes be confusing for others.

Patti has been a dear friend of mine for years. We often get together for lunch to catch up. At our last lunch she said, "I missed you," even though it had been only a week since we had last seen each other.

I said, "Okay."

My lackluster response was not what she expected. There was a brief, uncomfortable silence.

"Well, didn't you miss me too?"

"No, not really. I seldom miss people when I'm not with them."

I noticed a wounded look on her face. I do not like to disappoint anyone (I am more afraid of rejection than I am of death), but in order for me to have a close relationship with someone—a friend, coworkers, or my family—I have to be authentic and honest about who I really am. I have to be truthful, even if it's unusual or upsetting to some.

So I continued, "Patti, I know the normal expectation. I'm supposed to say that I missed you, when we have not been together for a while.

"Right. It lets me know that you care about me."

"Patti, I do care about you. And I show that by being totally present when I'm with you. Right here, right now. I'm sitting across from you in this restaurant, and you have my complete attention. I'm looking you in the eye and enjoying your company. I'm not thinking about problems at the office that came up this morning or the disasters that I may face this afternoon. I've turned off the sound on my cell phone so I'm not going to be distracted by calls or texts. I won't look at my BlackBerry until we've said, 'Goodbye.' I'm not thinking about my children, what Daveen is doing, or how my stock investments are performing. I always want to get the most I can from our time together, which is why I'm focusing on you, right here, right now."

"That I like."

"But it goes both ways. When I'm not with you, when I'm writing or teaching or meeting with an investor, I'm paying close attention to something or someone else—my own thoughts, my students, or whomever I'm with at that time.

"I guess maybe you're right, but it doesn't feel normal that you don't miss someone you care about when you are not with them."

"I agree. My approach isn't customary. But maybe the reason that we are such good friends is because we are so fully present when we are with each other. Our 'apartness' makes our 'togetherness' more precious."

She smiled and nodded.

I experienced the exact opposite many years ago, in line to greet a celebrity after a reception. The experienced guest of honor greeted everyone in a way that was so mechanical that it felt meaningless.

When it was my turn to greet him, he looked directly at me and said, "Glad to see you," while shaking the hand of the person in front of me. He then took my hand, pulled me along, and said, "Glad to see you," to the person behind me. When he talked to me he was shaking the hand of the person in front of me, and when he held my hand he was talking to the person in back of me while moving me out of the way. I felt like a bag of stale bread, not a human being, to be disposed of as efficiently as possible.

We all need to feel special. We need to feel that people are paying attention to us. I recall the final soliloquy from the Arthur Miller play, *Death of a Salesman*. The salesman, Willy Loman, has taken his own life, partly because he was snubbed when his employer of many years found him no longer useful. No one returned his calls and Willy felt like a failure.

At the end of the play his widow says, "But he's a human being, and a terrible thing is happening to him. So attention must be paid."

Each of us feels discounted when we fail to receive full attention. When he was seven years old I accompanied my son Craig to his monthly cub scout meeting. I was bored, so I sat in back and read *Time* magazine. After each meeting Craig complained bitterly.

"Dad, please sit in front and watch me."

I continued to sit in the back. I hope that if I had a chance to relive this today I would do it differently. Craig seems to pay full attention to his young sons.

In any relationship, any real relationship, attention must be paid.

PEOPLE TOOL
FOR LOVE & RELATIONSHIPS
3

FINDING A RELATIONSHIP—
BE PREPARED

When we stop to think, we often miss our opportunity.
—PUBLILIUS SYRUS
Maxim 185

Who ever loved that loved not at first sight.
—CHRISTOPHER MARLOWE
Hero and Leander, the First Sestiad (1598)

The distance from "me" to "us" may be as far away as a star in the nighttime sky or as close as your inbox. Part of the charm of life is that you will never know in advance whether, or when, the love of your life will enter from stage left or stage right. I hope this chapter and those that follow will help you to make "us" more likely to happen, and happen soon.

Harry, a very close friend of mine, was looking for a woman to share his life with. He looked when he was eighteen. He looked when he was twenty-five. He was still looking when he was forty. I thought that Harry was going to remain a lifelong bachelor.

One day Harry met Suva at a business conference. Their eyes locked and they began to talk. Four hours later they were still lost in conversation. That happened when he was forty-two. Harry and Suva have now been married for seven years and are raising two active young children. It might take years to find the other half of your "us," but you can know it in an instant.

I, for one, believe in "love at first sight." And you should believe, at the very least, in "like at first sight." I've been married three times and each of these significant relationships began at first sight.

I still remember the moment when Jo Anne Wolfe (I kid you not) walked into room 357 at John Marshall High School. I was a senior and captain of the debate team. She was a junior and interested in joining the speech club. I said to myself, "Yes! I can do this," and volunteered to help her. After our first date she asked me to the "Sadie Hawkins" dance. Five years later we were married, and Jo Anne became a real Fox.

I also remember the day I met my second wife, Susan. I was thirty-two and we were both at a weekend workshop for singles. The minute I saw her sitting barefoot on the floor I said, to myself, "I could marry that woman." Within seven months we were husband and wife.

I met my present wife, Daveen, at a bookstore where she worked. I was a customer and first saw her out of the corner of my eye while she was sitting at her desk. I thought to myself, "I don't know if she is married, single, or has ten children, but I'd sure like to meet her." You know the end of that story.

My experience with love at first sight doesn't stop with me. When I was in law school a fellow student asked me after our Criminal Law class, "Who was that cute girl you were talking to in front of the law school yesterday?"

"Her name is Irene," I said, "and we've been friends since we were six."

"She seems really nice. I'd like to meet her. How do I get in touch?"

"I'll have to ask her first." And I did. She was interested, I gave him her phone number, and four years later they were married.

My purpose is not to praise the virtues of love (or liking someone) at first sight. I do point out, however, that the single, most important relationship of your life might begin today, and in the most unlikely manner. So you should always be open to that possibility, because the love or your life might very well want to meet you in school, at work, or over the Internet.

Of course, before you fully commit to anyone, I hope you will take the time to enjoy their company in many different settings and get to know them well. Appearances, as we all know, can sometimes be misleading. One story from my past illustrates this.

Years ago, Sammy, the newspaper vendor in my neighborhood, stacked up a small mountain of Sunday newspapers to sell on the corner of Fountain Avenue and Hillhurst every Saturday evening. He always greeted me with a smile and a cheerful word as he handed me my Sunday *Los Angeles Times*.

"Beautiful night," he would say. Or, "Have a great day tomorrow." He was so pleasant and apparently charming that I often went out of my way to buy my newspaper from him. Sammy must have sold a thousand newspapers every Saturday evening.

One afternoon I was shopping a few blocks away when a black Cadillac squealed to a stop. Sammy leaped out and raced to a nearby newspaper vending machine. The coin box was stuck, and Sammy, who was obviously there to collect the coins, began kicking it and shouting curse words. Could this be my Sammy? The same sweet, cheerful guy who sold me my Sunday newspaper?

I looked more closely and, yes, it was him.

I never went out of my way to buy a newspaper from him again. He appeared to be a very nice man when he was selling papers, but he was angry and had a nasty temper when he thought no one was watching.

To find a relationship, put a smile on your face and keep it there. Be happy and be prepared, and I mean all of the time, because you never know when you'll meet the other part of your "us." Go skiing. Take a class. Participate in activities you enjoy. Have fun. Be open and available, and when you meet someone, take time to get know him or her so that an enduring "us" will have time to bond.

As Tony sings in *Westside Story*, "Something's coming, something good."

PEOPLE TOOL
FOR LOVE & RELATIONSHIPS
4

HOW TO BE
THE RIGHT PERSON

To be loved, be loveable.
—OVID
Ars Amatoria, Book II

Love to faults is always blind,
Always is to joy inclin'd,
Lawless, wing'd and unconfin'd,
And breaks all chains from every mind.
—WILLIAM BLAKE
Poem, "Love to Faults," from Blake's *Notebook*

My childhood fairy tale was to grow up, fall in love, get married, and live happily ever after. My parents were married for more than fifty years. When I was young I seldom heard a harsh word between them. Mom and Dad seemed to prove that the fairy tale was real.

Alas, for me, after ten years of marriage to my high school sweetheart, Jo Anne, the "happily ever after" part was shredded by conflict.

Then I met Jill. We lived "happily ever after" for three years.

Next I met and married Susan. It took four years for "happily ever after" to fade into a vague memory.

After three failed attempts at "happily ever after," I began to realize that the problem was not Susan. Or Jo Anne. Or Jill. The problem was me. At that point I decided it was more important for me to *be* the right person than for me to *find* the right person.

Today I realize that in order to build a relationship that lasts I need to put more energy into *being* the right person than into *finding* the right person. And it has worked. I have now been married to Daveen for almost thirty-five years.

How do I seek to "be" the right person in a relationship?

1. I have to be authentic. I don't pretend to be someone I'm not for the sake of winning favor. I don't act as if I want to travel if, in reality, what I really want to do at the end of each day is fall asleep in my own bed.

2. I recognize I am not the right person for everyone. While I don't believe there's only one ideal person out there for each of us, I do believe there are many people who are not right for each other. Wine and talcum powder just don't mix.

3. I need a partner who is authentic with me. Daveen was recently at the wedding of Bob and Ellen. Immediately after the ceremony Bob's new "one and only" (but not for very long) said to him, "Now I never have to set foot on your damned sailboat again." Neither Daveen nor I harbor any dream to own a sailboat. In fact, she says we are "camping out" when the hotel does not have twenty-four hour room service.

4. We each need to be clear about our needs and expectations. Thirty-five years ago, before my wife and I were married, I asked her if she wanted to continue working after we married. Whatever choice she made was fine with me, and she said that she would prefer to stay at home to raise our children. I have a friend, however, who told me that when he and his bride returned from their honeymoon she announced, to his dismay, "I quit my job and expect you to support us." The problem

was that he needed two more years to complete law school.

5. I practice the art of compromise with a smile. I know that Daveen does not find me to be perfect, nor do I expect her to be. We are not able to provide each other with everything we want, and we've learned over the years to compromise with each other . . . and do it with a smile.

6. I look at the positives in our marriage through a telescope. I look at the negatives through the "wrong" end of the telescope.

7. We each have outside interests and friendships. Few people do well together 24/7, even on the beach in Hawaii, and we do not have to be everything for one another all of the time.

In order to give life direction and meaning, each of us needs a dream. But to help our dream of "happily ever after" come true, we must seek not only to *find* the right person, but also to *be* the right person.

PACE YOURSELF

Human relationships don't belong to engineering, mathematics, chess, which offer problems that can be perfectly solved. Human relationships grow, like trees.

—J.B. Priestley and Jacquetta Hawkes
Journey Down a Rainbow

This porridge is not too hot and not too cold.
This porridge is just right.
—Fairy tale of "Goldilocks and the Three Bears"

When I was in high school a friend of mine, Peter, was a member of the track team. His event was the mile run.

Peter usually finished toward the back of the pack, with a personal best time of just under six minutes. Before the final meet of the season Peter pulled me aside and said, "Alan, I figured it out. Any decent high school miler should be able to run the mile in five minutes or less. Watch me today. I'm going to cut forty-five seconds off of my personal best and finish in five minutes."

Peter was smart. He was the only member of our class to attend Cal Tech after graduation. But smart does not necessarily mean correct. At the end of the first lap Peter led the entire pack by five yards. After the second lap he was still hanging on to second place. By the end of the third lap Pete had dropped to third, but, with a strong finish, still had a chance to meet his goal of a five-minute mile. Then, with three quarters of a lap to go, he ran out of energy. Sitting in the stands I cringed as Pete slowed to a jog, then to barely more than a walk. He was gasping for breath, and then Pete collapsed as he crossed the finish line. His time was seven minutes, by far his worst showing of the season.

The problem was in his pacing. Pete started too fast, and ended up last.

Pacing is also important when it comes to your search for a partner. A college friend of mine, Darren, always started too fast in his relationships. He would arrange for twenty-four red roses to arrive at the home of every woman he dated—before their first date. A bouquet of roses after a first date is romantic. But before a first date those same roses announce insecurity. As you can imagine, Darren had very few second dates. By starting out too fast, in a sense, he finished last.

If you are looking for a one-night stand, you might want to run as fast as you possibly can. But if you are looking for a continuing relationship, an "us," you have to pace yourself.

When you meet someone who might be "us" material, relax. Focus on simply enjoying your time together. Don't repeatedly ask yourself, "Would he be good in bed?" or "What would my family think of her," or even, "I wonder if she's free next Saturday night?" That's putting the trailer before the truck. What matters most is this: are you having a good time in the moment?

When I was single at age thirty-five, I often attended a singles meeting in Topanga Canyon in hopes of meeting a special woman. I was shy. The first Friday evening I parked my car, walked up the steps to the front door, and froze. I turned, sprinted down the stairs, and dashed back to my car and home. The following Friday I worked up enough courage to actually open the front door of the house and join the group.

Each week I saw men "working the room," harvesting four or five telephone numbers. But I just couldn't do that. So I decided I would aim for a goal that I could achieve—to simply have a good time. And if I talked to one woman I liked I would ask for her phone number. If she said "no" I would still enjoy my evening.

Soon I made that my goal for every first date: get to know her, and have a good time. I must admit that on a second date, I did hope for a good night kiss. I paced myself, and it worked for me.

Exactly what pace you should take really depends on the circumstances. Should you text or call the next morning or wait a week? If you're the woman, should you contact him? That depends on you, on him or her, and on your chemistry. Go with your instinct and your heart. Don't be too eager, but don't be too reserved. Be willing to find a tempo that works for both of you. As Goldilocks might say, "not too fast, and not too slow, but just right."

I've read the story of a high school cross-country team in Boulder, Colorado, that typically ran three-mile races. The team achieved little success until a new coach brought with him a fresh idea.

The coach did not train his team to aim simply for a faster time, like my friend Pete had attempted in his one-mile fiasco. In fact, the new coach didn't care about how well his team ran during the first two miles. Instead, he trained his runners to focus on how many place positions they could improve during the final mile. He considered a runner who was in sixth place at the end of the second mile and in third place at the end of the race to be a success. After a few years his team won the state championship by living the team motto: "We run best at the end."

I like that. "We run best at the end." That is what your journey from "me" to "us" is all about—pacing yourself, not pushing too hard at the beginning, and leaving something in reserve for your astonishing days to come.

PEOPLE TOOL
6
FOR LOVE & RELATIONSHIPS

HER:
HAPPINESS = EXPECTATIONS – REALITY

Happiness lies in the consciousness we have of it.
—GEORGE SAND
Handsome Lawrence

*To be without some of the things you want
is an indispensable part of happiness.*
—BERTRAND RUSSELL
The Conquest of Happiness

What is happiness? Many great minds have offered various answers to this perennial question. I, for one, think that it can be boiled down to a simple Happiness Equation: Happiness equals Your Own Expectations minus Your Perception of Reality, or HER for short.

For example, suppose you expect an inheritance of ten thousand dollars from your favorite aunt, and when her will is read you actually receive a bequest of thirty thousand dollars. That's twenty thousand dollars more than you expected, which is twenty thousand dollars of happiness. The first ten thousand was expected.

But if you anticipate that your aunt will leave you three hundred thousand dollars and her gift is only one hundred thousand, you may have two hundred thousand dollars of disappointment, or unhappiness, despite the fact that you actually receive seventy thousand dollars more than in the first example.

It then follows that there are two ways to increase your happiness. First, you can improve your reality. Second, you can reduce your expectations. I find the second to be easier and just as successful a way to bring happiness into my life.

Ten years into my commercial real estate career, one of my investors asked me, "Why do your projections for my investments always seem to perform better than you anticipate? You predict a return of five percent on my money, and I usually receive six."

This was a reasonable question, and I gave him a reasonable answer:

"To invest in real estate, you have to be optimistic. But to stay in it for the long haul, and in order to avoid losing your entire wardrobe, you have to be realistic. As an optimist I might predict a return of eight percent. But as a realist I know there will always be unexpected problems. The roof will leak, or a recession will hit. So I always forecast a slightly lower return than I believe the marketplace will deliver.

"I want you, as an investor, to be pleased with your investment. But I'm not just providing you with a successful investment. I am helping to create happiness. If the actual investment performance is better than you expect, you are going to be happy."

The investor continued to invest with me, happily, for many years.

This is a good example of how the Happiness Equation works in business. But it applies just as well in a personal relationship.

Each of us enters a new relationship with high expectations. It's like putting your nickel into a slot machine in Las Vegas when you believe you have the possibility of receiving a jackpot. Why not? Why not enter a new relationship with the expectation that it will be outstanding or, at the very least, better than the last one?

The problem is that if your initial expectation is unrealistic, your new friend or partner will then inevitably fall short, and you will be disappointed. In financial terms this is like earning a profit of six percent on your last investment, but expecting a return of twenty percent on your new one.

If your expectations are too high your partner will inevitably fail to live up to the vision of sugarplums dancing in your head. This is not a recipe for happiness.

We all want to be saved. I want my doctor to prescribe a pill or give me a shot, and then presto! I am cured. I want my attorney to write a letter and make my legal trouble disappear. I want my partner in life to anticipate all of my needs and meet them before I even know what they are. But when I allow these *wants* to rise to the level of expectations, beware! High expectations are like the *Titanic*, destined to strike an iceberg and potentially sink your entire relationship.

To enter into a relationship you need to be an optimist. To stay in and enjoy that relationship, you need to be a realist.

One of my favorite movies is *Pretty Woman*. This is a fairy tale in which Richard Gere, a modern-day Prince Charming, climbs a fire escape and asks Julia Roberts, "So what happens after he climbs up and rescues her?"

"She rescues him right back."

This movie is a romantic comedy filled with promise. And in the real world you and your partner will indeed help to rescue each other. But it's important to remember that, in the end, each of us is responsible for his or her own liberation.

So I suggest you test the HER equation. Keep your expectations lower than what you think is realistic. No one will be Princess or Prince Charming all of the time. Your relationship cannot always be perfect. But you can enjoy and celebrate the reality of each other for many long and happy years. This is as close to living a fairy tale as any of us should ever expect.

PEOPLE TOOL
7
FOR LOVE & RELATIONSHIPS

CORE VALUES

Be so true to thyself, as thou be not false to others.

—FRANCIS BACON
Essays
"Of Wisdom for a Man's Self" (1665)

It is only with the heart that one can see rightly;
what is essential is invisible to the eye.

—ANTOINE DE SAINT-EXUPÉRY
The Little Prince

When I was young, I realized that I had a short list of issues on which I was not willing to compromise. Psychologists describe these nonnegotiable areas as "core values."

On the other hand, I realized that in order to get along well with other people I would need to be as flexible as possible on everything else. I have never seen a joyful relationship in which one person insists they have to win, or be right, every single time.

I'm happy to let you choose the restaurant, the movie, or the destination for our vacation. I will always find somewhere to eat or amuse myself in the lobby if I don't like the movie, and, if necessary, I can remain in our room and read books or write for a week on any vacation. On these issues I'm flexible.

But there are other areas in which I am not so accommodating. For example, I will not accept physical or emotional bullying. I worry about your safety and will insist that you stay in touch—no disappearing from my radar for an entire night, or even for two or three hours, when I expect to see you. These are matters I will not negotiate. The same is, or should be, true for most of us.

Before she agreed to marry me, Daveen said, "I don't cook." This was a subject on which she was not willing to change her position. I'm glad she brought it up and, even though I was disappointed, we agreed that she would not have to cook. Of course, today I sometimes tease her because over the years Daveen has prepared many excellent melted cheese sandwiches for me, which are always my fallback for a tasty breakfast, lunch, or dinner.

Miranda, a close friend of mine, married for the first time when she was thirty-eight years old. At the time this surprised me because she had always demonstrated a clear pattern of ignoring her own core values in her relationships with men. She would call me and enthusiastically describe her latest boyfriend. Then she would tell me, in some detail, a specific characteristic about him that troubled her, such as the fact that he smoked, and conclude that the relationship would not last more than a few weeks. But six months later, in spite of her initial misgiving, they would be living together. And, predictably, several years after that she would leave him, always for the same fault that had troubled her in the beginning. As I said, Miranda ignored her own core values.

Your core values are unique to you. Perhaps you need to share with your partner the same religion or political beliefs. You may insist on living in an environment where everything is in its place—no dirty socks on the bedroom floor. Your potential partner may have very different ideas about having, or raising, children. One of my core values is that I will not be with anyone who drinks regularly or heavily.

Before you enter into a serious relationship, or any relationship that you hope will last, it's important to identify your core values and discuss them with your prospective partner. For example, Daveen has many friends, and she likes to attend their weddings. I find the prospect of going to a party where I don't know anyone to be quite uncomfortable. Daveen and I had a clash of core values on this issue, so before we were married we agreed that I would join her at one wedding of her choice every three years. Ironically, at one of those weddings I met a man who presented to me the best real estate investment of my entire career.

Inevitably, every couple will have some differences in core values. You might want to know, for example, in the handling of money, is your partner a saver or a spender? Or, will you be more important to your partner than his or her friends or family of origin? And the big one, of course: who will be the one in charge of the TV remote control?

I hate unpleasant surprises. That's why I want to know, in advance, which of my own core values might become an issue for my partner.

If a conflict of core values does arise later in your relationship, and it might, talk it through. Hopefully, you can reach a solution that will satisfy both of you. Daveen and I enjoy art, but our tastes occasionally differ. This is why we have agreed that either of us can remove from the walls of our home any specific work of art that one of us dislikes.

A conflict in core values is like an unstoppable force ramming an immovable object. Thunk! Your relationship can be badly damaged or destroyed. The choice is yours. Figure out those issues that you can't compromise on, and discuss them early in a new relationship. Then you'll know if it's possible to move forward, with each of your core values firmly in place, and without inviting an inevitable and difficult conflict or separation.

PEOPLE TOOL
FOR LOVE & RELATIONSHIPS
8

IS IT SAFE?

Oh the comfort—the inexpressible comfort of feeling safe with a person, having neither to weigh thoughts, nor measure words, but pouring them all right out, just as they are, chaff and grain together; certain that a faithful hand will take and sift them— keep what is worth keeping—and with the breath of kindness blow the rest away.

—DINAH MULOCK CRAIK
A Life for a Life

The average man doesn't want to be free. He wants to be safe.

—H.L. MENCKEN
Notes on Democracy

In the 1976 movie *The Marathon Man*, there is a scene in which the hero "Babe" Levy, played by Dustin Hoffman, is being tortured with a dental drill by a demented dentist, played by Laurence Olivier, while strapped to a high chair. As Olivier is drilling into Hoffman's teeth, he keeps repeating the question "Is it safe?"

Is *what* safe? Hoffman's character doesn't have a clue what the dentist is talking about. To him, it looks like "bye-bye" teeth.

I'm going to turn this scene around and apply it to the realm of relationships. How many times does someone ask you, "Is it safe?" or "Are you safe for me?" when you don't even know that they are asking the question?

I'll give you an example.

On our second date, my yet-to-be second wife, Susan, and I were talking on the sofa in her living room. I suggested that we stop talking for a while, and within seconds Susan flew into my arms and we began to kiss. When it looked as if it might become even more physical Susan stopped, looked up at me, and said, "What religion are you?"

I told her, and I asked her what religion she was. She told me, and then asked if I was very religious.

"No. Just moderately. How about you?"

"The same."

We now knew we shared the same religious orientation and that we were both sensible about it.

Our physical relationship progressed.

The next time we were together I said, "So you wanted to know whether or not it was safe to let yourself go a little more with me."

"No."

"Then why did you ask about my religion after we started to kiss?"

"Oh, I don't know. I was just curious."

I think Susan believed that. But I didn't, because her timing was too unusual. I believe that she was really asking, "Is it safe to get involved with you?" And while she was moderately religious, it was important to her that whomever she was with be the same.

Learning to find the deeper meaning in your partner's words is challenging. But it is essential if you expect to develop deeper trust and understanding. This is especially important in situations where you or your partner express anger at a time, or in a way, that seems untimely or inappropriate to the situation.

My friend Tom told me that a week before he was planning to propose to his long-term girlfriend Celia, he offered to give her his old cell phone because he had bought a new one. Celia responded by email.

"How dare you offer me your used phone. I have the same kind and it works just fine. I don't want your hand-me-downs."

Tom was shocked and felt rejected, but instead of retaliating he wrote back to Celia, "Thanks for letting me know. I'm glad you already have a cell phone that you like. I only want the best for you."

Two days later Celia admitted to him, "I was scared that you were getting too close, and if I accepted another gift from you, I would be somehow obligated. I've thought about it and want you to know I'm sorry. I love you."

When Tom did propose to her a short time after, Celia's answer was an enthusiastic, "Yes!"

Freud writes, "Sometimes a cigar is just a cigar." Sometimes a cigar is exactly what it seems to be and does not represent anything else. Likewise, behavior is often just what it appears to be.

But I suggest that you look for the times when a partner might really be asking, "Is it safe?" In those moments when he or she appears to be rejecting you, they may really be asking for your reassurance.

Last week I visited with Carolyn, an eye surgeon. She told me that a man she really liked had recently said that he wanted to spend more time apart.

"Is he afraid of you?" I asked.

She hesitated.

"I think so. Yes."

"Talk to him about it. Maybe you can help him realize that you're human too, and even though you're successful he doesn't have to be afraid of you. You need him, too."

Carolyn smiled. "I'll give it a try."

You should always listen for the music behind the words, and pay attention to the song as well as the lyrics. Often your partner may be scared, but unwilling to admit it, and is really asking you: "Is it safe?"

TRUTH IS THE LONG CUT

When in doubt, tell the truth.

—MARK TWAIN
Following the Equator
"Pudd'nhead Wilson's New Calendar"

If you once forfeit the confidence of your fellow citizens, you can never regain their respect and esteem. It is true that you may fool all of the people some of the time, you can even fool some of the people all of the time, but you can't fool all of the people all the time.

—ABRAHAM LINCOLN
Quoted in *Lincoln's Yarns and Stories* by Alexander K. McClure

A lie is a shortcut.

When I was a kid I lied a lot. The reason was simple. When I did something my father disapproved of I would be punished, whether I admitted my misdeed or not. There was no plea-bargaining in the Fox household. A confession was not rewarded by a reduced sentence, so I never confessed. And even though I was caught about eighty percent of the time, my lies helped me to avoid the inevitable punishment for one act of misconduct in five.

Many of the behaviors we begin in childhood become habits that continue for a lifetime. If you're like me and regularly told lies as a child, it is likely that you will act in exactly the same way as an adult.

But you have three choices. If you like the habit of lying, if you think it's a winner, you can choose to continue it. If you don't like that habit, you can choose to change it (which may be easier said than done). Or if you don't like the habit you can choose to put it to a better use.

For example, the Nobel Prize-winning author Israel Bashevis Singer wrote, "When I was a child they called me a liar. Now they call me a writer."

Hmmmm. I like that idea. Part of the time I am a writer. I make things up. When friends recognize themselves in one of the characters I write about they often say, "That sounds nice, but it's not what I really said."

They are probably correct, because while I have an excellent memory for emotions, I do not remember exact words from a conversation. So in writing I do not transcribe conversations. I recreate them. Am I a liar? Not at all. I am a writer. Israel Bashevis Singer said so.

But the part of my life where I am not a writer is the much larger part. It includes relationships in the here and now and people with whom I have business and personal connections. In this area of my life, I never take the shortcut of a lie. Instead, I take the long cut of the truth.

I am a pragmatist. And I choose to tell the truth on practical grounds. You may choose to tell the truth simply because it is moral.

I decided in my early twenties that in business I would always tell the truth. I aimed for long-term relationships, and I didn't want to jeopardize any new partnership by being "caught" in a lie. I may have made a lot more deals if I had exaggerated to my potential investors and said, "Your cash return will be seven percent." But by taking the long cut of the truth and letting them know that it should be a more realistic five percent, I stay out of trouble and avoid lawsuits. I believe that over the course of a career the long cut of the truth is more effective than the shortcut of a lie. It's similar to the tortoise beating the hare in an extended race.

In personal relationships I have reached the same conclusion, although for an even more important reason. In a personal relationship the truth is even more crucial than it is in business because we have fewer personal relationships—they are more rare and precious. It's much easier to locate a new customer than a new friend to replace one of twenty years, or to locate a new spouse.

When I was eight or nine years old I was walking home from school one afternoon when I spied a pumpkin patch on a vacant lot. I plucked a large ripe pumpkin from its vine and lugged it home with me.

When my father returned from work he said, "Where did you get that pumpkin?"

I lied. "I got it from the people who had a lot of pumpkins next to their house. They gave it to me, Dad."

"Did you ask them if you could have it?"

"Sure, Dad."

"Take me there and show me," he said.

My short life flashed before my eyes as my dad escorted me to the vacant lot. He went up to the front door of the nearest house and rang the bell.

Picture a young boy sitting on the sidewalk, staring down at his feet and holding his head in his hands.

Punishment followed, even though the man in the house told my dad he would have been happy to give me the pumpkin. The problem was that I hadn't asked and lied to my dad when I told him that I had. Dad didn't trust me for years.

One day a former business associate of mine discovered a large assortment of boxes hidden in his wife's closet. He soon found out that she had been secretly using her credit card on shopping sprees to purchase items she knew they couldn't afford. She had been hiding her shopping addiction from him for some time. Not long after this discovery they were divorced.

Years ago Daveen received a telephone call from a credit card company to tell her that she had exceeded the credit limit on her card.

There was just one problem. The credit card wasn't hers. Apparently our nanny had diverted a credit card application that came in the mail, applied for the card in Daveen's name, and ran up six thousand dollars in charges while intercepting the monthly bills. This was not only a lie, but also a crime. We immediately fired the nanny and filed a police report. This was an extreme example of a lie of omission being as destructive as, or worse than, a lie of commission.

The shortcut of a lie can often be tempting. If you lie, maybe you will get away with more than I did when I was a boy. But sooner or later the lie may catch up to you as it almost always did with me. In the meantime, you will experience tremendous stress, always worrying that your lie might be discovered. And if it is, you will certainly lose someone's trust, and you may also lose an important relationship

Instead, I suggest that you, personally and in business, take the long cut of truth. And if your friend or partner doesn't, you might then consider the shortcut of finding a different friend or partner. (You might want to look up the relevant People Tool of "Patterns Persist" that is described in my first *People Tools* book.)

PEOPLE TOOL
10
FOR LOVE & RELATIONSHIPS

MY MANY AND ONLY

*If you can't be with the one you love,
Love the one you're with.*

—STEPHEN STILLS
"Love the One You're With." Song (1970)

*They that do change old love for new,
Pray gods, they change for worse!*

—GEORGE PEELE
The Arraignment of Paris (1584)

Have you found your "one and only?" If you haven't, I wish you the best. But if you have, how do you know for sure?

I'm in the business of answering questions, especially my own. My answer to "How do you know for sure" is "You don't, and you never will."

I believe that any of us could be perfectly happy, such as it is given to us to be perfectly happy, with any one of more than ten thousand partners. And how will you ever know whether the partner you have or the partner you may find is number one, number three hundred twenty-three, or number ten thousand? You never will know for sure, if only because you can't give each one of them a try. Believe me on this. I've probably tried more than most.

I met my first wife when we were both sixteen. We divorced at age thirty-one, with three children. She was my first "one and only."

My second wife was wonderful. For five years she was my smart and beautiful, but incompatible, new one and only.

My present wife, Daveen, and I also have three children. She is my sexy and "still getting to know you" one and only. She has been this for more than thirty-four years and will be (hopefully) for thirty more.

And yet . . . if only I knew for sure where Daveen stands on that list of ten thousand potential partners. Is she number two thousand four hundred and seven, or number six, or number two? Maybe I could continue to search for my number one, only to discover that she is already married and living in Anchorage, Alaska.

And how do you know where you stand on your partner's list? Maybe he or she really is number one for you, but you are number one million and sixteen for them. I know, I know. You are you and therefore must be number one on the list of every woman or man you love, ever have loved, or ever will love. If only they realized that, they would be completely delighted simply to bask in your presence every single day and cater to your every whim. "Yes, dear," would be their only reply whenever you asked. For anything. Daveen often says, "Yes, dear." And that's when I start running for cover.

(Daveen just read this chapter. She said, "When I say 'yes, dear,' it's an attack. When you say 'yes, dear' it's self-defense." She also said she wants credit for being self-aware. My reply here, for all to see, is, "Yes, dear. Of course, dear.")

Current research indicates that those who are the happiest in relationships are those who work at it. They talk to each other. They read books. They seek help. They think about what they need to change. They don't believe, as I did at age thirteen, that you merely have to find your "one and only," marry him or her, and live happily ever after. As a child I read *Grimm's Fairy Tales* by flashlight under the covers after my bedtime. I loved fairy tales then. I still do. But life is a lot more Grimm than those fairy tales, and life doesn't always have a happy ending.

Relationships are not well written and carefully edited. Relationships are always changing and can be messy. And successful relationships are a lot of work. Some days it may seem easier to move to Butte, Montana, and start searching for Mr. or Ms. Better there. But is that really the answer?

As I've said before, one of my favorite movies is *Pretty Woman*. Julia Roberts, I love you. We haven't yet met, but we've never had a fight. You've never been "too tired." You're very high on my "many and only" list, Julia. You're drop-dead gorgeous. You're a great actress. Call me. Email me. Please. If you're still married, leave him. Let's give it a try.

But if I were to leave my wife for Julia, or any other woman, the bottom line is that once reality replaces fantasy, I would still have to do the work to make that new relationship thrive. I think it's a better choice to invest in the relationship I already have.

Daveen, I love you. Not just because I want brownie points, which I always do, and not just because you've put up with me for more than half your life, but also because you're almost always an excellent companion, you still love sex, and we're still both working at getting to know ourselves and each other. And most importantly, we have both committed to being the best partners we can be to each other, even knowing that there might be others out there that could possibly be higher on our list! Well, my list anyway. I know I'm perfect for you.

What could be more fun than working on your present relationship.

Nothing could be more fun. Except . . . maybe . . . Julia?

PEOPLE TOOL
11
FOR LOVE & RELATIONSHIPS

WITH ALL FAULTS

And that's the way it is.
—WALTER CRONKITE'S SIGN-OFF SENTENCE,
CBS Evening News

Men are so romantic, don't you think? They look for a perfect partner when what they should be looking for is perfect love.
—FAYE WELDON
The Sunday Times, September 6, 1987

I've worked in the real estate business for nearly fifty years. Occasionally I see a listing for a property to be sold "W.A.F.," which means "With All Faults." This is not very common because few people are eager to buy a property that will need a lot of work. Most of us would prefer to purchase a home that has been thoroughly inspected and has had all baseline improvements completed by the seller before we take possession.

With a relationship you don't have the same choice, because every human being on Earth has faults, and they are not so easily improved. I'm sure this is true even of the Dalai Lama, Mother Teresa, and Mahatma Gandhi. Of course, even if the perfect person did come along I see no reason why he or she would bother to strike up a conversation with you or me, because they would certainly find us to be less than perfect.

So you can either hide in a cave all by yourself or live with people who are faulty. I choose to live with people who, like me, have flaws. In relationships, it's always W.A.F.

I've heard it said that you accept your friends despite their faults and your intimate partners including their faults. I think that's an important distinction.

My friend Linda is very picky. It takes her five minutes to order lunch from any restaurant menu, even if she is a regular. I can accept that trait in a friend I see infrequently. But I couldn't put up with a life partner who agonizes every day over each little decision.

I may get into trouble here (some consider that one of my faults is my willingness to be "too" outspoken), but I do not think that my wife Daveen is perfect. And she doesn't think that I am, either. I just asked her if I'm perfect and she didn't even hesitate before saying, "No, dear."

And yet, here we are, a long-married couple that has had almost thirty-five years to search out and destroy every single fault we can find in each other. Not surprisingly, we have both failed in that mission. And at this point I'm going to bet that we will never succeed. Perhaps Daveen's dying statement to me will be, "Be sure to pick up your socks."

Since I am a practicing pragmatist, when Daveen displays a flaw there is only one fundamental question: Is our marriage on or off?

If the relationship is off, one of us will move out carrying with him, or her, all clothing, personal possessions, and defects. That is a slick solution, until the next fault-infested human moves in.

If the relationship is on, I then embrace the Serenity Prayer (written by the American theologian Reinhold Niebuhr). "God, grant me the serenity to accept the things I cannot change, the courage to change the things I can, and the wisdom to know the difference."

Ah, "the wisdom to know the difference."

Ah, "the serenity to accept the things I cannot change."

I say that you and your partner begin every intimate relationship W.A.F., even if one of you—the other one, of course—is more faulty than you are. So accept the situation, focus on the positive, and enjoy the best relationship you possibly can.

During the Los Angeles riots of 1992, which caused 53 deaths, 2,383 injuries, and more than 7,000 fires, Rodney King appeared on television and issued his legendary plea, "Can we all get along?"

Thanks for the tip. It's now more than twenty years later, and as a society and individuals we're still working on it, Rodney. We're still working on it.

SHARE

Love consists in this, that two solitudes know,
and touch, and protect each other.
—RANIER MARIA RILKE
Letters to a Young Poet
Translated by M.D. Herter Norton

Love is sharing and caring.
—ALAN C. FOX

In the late 1970s, when I was married to Susan, the economic cycle turned down and my cash reserves fell off a cliff.

I was quite unhappy at the time, and although I always prefer to shield my family from my own anxiety when cash runs low, my wife Susan must have suspected my concern.

One morning as I was preparing to leave for work, she asked me to sit down and talk with her for a minute. Even though I was already in "work mode," I agreed. She took my hands and said, "Alan, I know that you've been concerned about money, and this morning you seem especially distracted."

"Well, it has been a problem for a while."

"I've put away forty thousand dollars of savings in my own account, and I'd be happy to give it to you."

I felt the way I imagine my father did when I was eight years old and used my entire life savings of seven dollars and fifty cents to treat my family to dinner at a restaurant.

"Susan, I really appreciate your offer."

"I mean it. You can have it."

"Thank you so much. I really do appreciate your offer, but it's better for you to keep your money. If I can't solve my cash flow problem soon myself, then we may need your savings to live on. I don't think that will happen, but it might. And I could run through all of your money by ten a.m. this morning and still be short. I appreciate your offer. I really do. I love you."

It was as if Susan's arms were still around me as a drove to the office to face my business reality. I felt comforted, because there was someone I shared my life with who really cared. This is the stuff of which an "us" is made.

When my friend Brenda was fifty years old, she fell deeply in love with Art. She peppered him with texts and emails every day. Because she worked in Los Angeles and he was a Chicago lawyer, they spent only weekends together. Every week or two, one of her texts would say something like, "I love you so much. I hope you never leave me."

When they were together, Art would reassure her. One Sunday morning he said, "Brenda, I love you. And I'm not going to leave you."

"I know, but when I'm by myself during the week I get scared. It's strange. I've had other relationships, but I've never been so scared before."

"Have I done something to make you feel this way?"

"No, not at all."

"Then why do you feel different about me? Why are you afraid?"

Brenda hesitated.

"Because you are the love of my life, and I feel that I love you more than you love me."

Art responded in the best possible way: He simply held her. I'm happy to report that they are still together today, six years later, and continue to be honest and vulnerable with one other. They have learned that the journey from "me" to "us" is an expedition filled with sharing and caring.

A close friend once wrote to me, "Suppose they gave a life and nobody came?"

You *do* have a life, right here and right now. And the "us" in it is found not only in the "me" of you living your own life, but also in the honest and deep sharing of that "me" with another "me," who is filled with every bit as much love, and every bit as much fear inside, as you.

YOU DON'T ALWAYS HAVE TO ANSWER THE TELEPHONE

The tragedy of love is indifference.
—SOMERSET MAUGHAM
The Trembling of a Leaf

I scarcely remember counting upon any Happiness—
I look not for it if it be not in the present moment.
—JOHN KEATS
Letter to Benjamin Bailey, November 22, 1817

When I was growing up we had one telephone in our home. My brother and I were instructed always to answer it after the second ring.

One afternoon when I was a teenager, the telephone rang at an inconvenient time. My mother said to me, "You don't have to answer it."

"But Mom . . ."

Maybe she was tired. Maybe she knew who was calling and didn't want to talk to the person. For whatever reason, Mom said, "Alan, you don't always have to answer the telephone."

I thought about this for years, and I now realize that my Mom's permission was a turning point in my life.

In any relationship it's crucial to pay attention to your partner. Not partial attention. Full attention. And that means that sometimes you should not answer your phone!

Today almost everyone carries a cell phone. My dad was honored recently at a concert at the University of Arizona. The provost of the university was sitting directly in front of him. In the middle of a cello solo Dad's cell phone rang. He answered it. I heard him say, not quietly, into the glow in his hand, "Not now!"

When his phone promptly rang again I suggested that he turn it off.

The question is this: Who is in charge of your life? Your parents? Your friends? Everyone who has your telephone number? Or you?

With a cell phone you have the advantage of knowing who is calling if their telephone number is in your list of contacts. But two of my close friends are "No Caller ID," as are thousands of other people whom I don't care to talk to. Do I have to answer my phone every time anyone dials my number?

I turn off my cell phone at meals, at movies, and after nine p.m. I also turn it off when I'm in the midst of a serious conversation.

Tom, a business associate, recently shared with me the reason he is no longer married to Rhonda, his high school sweetheart.

"Alan," he said, "she was always on the phone. One time we were on our way to a wedding, and Rhonda got a call less than a minute after we left the house. She was on her phone during the entire drive, and for ten minutes in the parking lot after we arrived. I couldn't get her off the phone. She finally said "goodbye" as we were standing in front of the church, and we ended up seating ourselves in the back row just as the ceremony started. It was embarrassing. And this happened all of the time. Whoever was on the other end of that telephone line was the center of Rhonda's attention. I felt like extra baggage."

I have a clear sense of my priorities. When my father, one hundred years old, calls me, I answer. When my wife calls, I almost always answer. If one of my children calls me during the business day, I either take their call or arrange to call them back. I refuse to elevate business to a higher priority in life than my family or close friends.

The quality of every relationship is directly related not only to the amount of time you spend together, but also, and more importantly, to the quality of that time. When you are on a date I don't think that you or your date would want your mother, or anyone else, to sit in the back seat. When we're together I don't want to be relegated to the back seat of your life while someone else has grabbed your full attention.

Give yourself a break from being plugged-in. You do not have to be available 24/7. Take to heart the aphorism "Good news will wait. Bad news will find you soon enough."

Part of me hates to say this, but you might even consider putting down this book and asking your partner to share with you the stories about his or her day.

And if your phone rings, you don't have to answer it. My mother gave you permission.

PEOPLE TOOL
FOR LOVE & RELATIONSHIPS
14

IT'S OKAY TO ASK

. . . it never does any harm to ask for what you want.
—JOSEPH WOOD KRUTCH
The Twelve Seasons: A Perpetual Calendar for the Country

Ask and it shall be given you.
—MATTHEW 7:7

Beliefs established in childhood tend to endure for a lifetime. Unfortunately, some of those beliefs have the potential to harm our relationships a great deal.

I grew up believing that it is not okay to ask.

When I wanted something, like a new bike or money to go to the movies, I would ask for what I wanted. Sometimes I asked my parents over and over and over again. I tried to wear at least one of my parents down until I got the answer I wanted. Every child tries this.

Understandably, my father wasn't able to provide everything I asked for, but he did not like to disappoint his family. To avoid having to repeatedly say "no" each time, he would almost always shout "NO" immediately and loudly. His voice thundered, and he seemed angry. Dad's big, loud "NO" frightened me, so I gradually stopped asking him for anything.

My reluctance to ask has continued into my adulthood (See the People Tool of "Mind Reading"). And as often happens, when I became a father myself I imitated my dad's behavior when his family asked him for something. When my children or my wife asked me for something I couldn't or didn't want to give them, I reacted with a loud and angry "NO." While my words said one thing, my underlying thought was, "I'm uncomfortable turning you down, so I'll try to discourage you from asking in the first place." Unconsciously, I hoped that my "NO" would block further requests so that I could avoid having to say "no" over and over and over again.

My technique worked well, just as it had for my father before me. My family stopped asking. But they also began to think of me as angry and withholding.

One day a therapist said to me, "Alan, it's okay to ask."

I was stunned and actually began to argue, "No it's not." But as the words left my mouth, I realized how ridiculous I sounded. Of course it's okay to ask. That's how we let others know what we want. That's how they let us know what they want. That's why the question mark was created.

I suddenly realized that for many years I had isolated myself from my family because of this single, long-held childhood belief. They were afraid of me. Having your family fear you may be convenient if you never want to have to say "no," but do you really want to terrorize your partner, your parents, and your children?

And do you want to live in fear of them?

So I decided to change. At work, and at home, when someone would say, "Uh, I'm not sure I should ask you this, but . . ." I got into the habit of interrupting and telling them, "It's always okay to ask." I even began to tell my family, "I'm glad you asked."

Not surprisingly, the atmosphere at home, and also at work, has become much more relaxed and comfortable.

Still, old habits die hard. To this day I'm reluctant to ask for something when I fear even a gentle "no." I don't like to ask for a different room when I register at a hotel or to ask a waiter to replace food when it's cold or salty. By comparison, Daveen has no problem asking anyone for anything. We've received many airline upgrades simply because she asked. Daveen even asks *me* for what she wants.

Incredible! And though I sometimes say no to her, most of the time I say yes!

When our daughter Sara, who wrote the foreword to this book, was in preschool, Daveen and I attended our first teacher conference.

"When Sara wants something, she asks for it," the teacher said. Daveen and I nodded approvingly.

"And if she doesn't get it, she asks again." The teacher now seemed a bit critical.

"That's great," I said, relieved that our daughter at age three was asking with much more assurance than I did.

"And then," the teacher concluded with a more than a trace of displeasure, "if she still doesn't get it, she asks someone else."

Go, Sara!

It's okay to ask. Really.

PUT ON YOUR OWN OXYGEN MASK FIRST

Caring for myself is not self-indulgence,
it is self-preservation . . .
—AUDRE LORDE
A Burst of Light: Essays

Love and compassion must begin with kindness toward ourselves.
—JACK KORNFIELD
The Art of Forgiveness, Lovingkindness, and Peace (2002)

Everyone who has traveled on a commercial airplane surely remembers the words, "In the event of a sudden loss in cabin pressure the oxygen masks will drop in front of you. Put on your own oxygen mask first, before helping your child or those around you."

That makes sense. How could I possibly help my eight-year-old child, or anyone else, if I am unconscious?

The same goes for relationships. In order for us to be a supportive partner, friend, or family member, we have to make sure that we are secure first. Often in our relationships we play the role of caretaker. We read books to our children at night so they will learn stories and absorb language skills. We console friends when they have lost a job or a relationship. We will take an entire week off from work to assist a deteriorating parent who has encountered sudden medical needs. We are happy to spend our own time and resources to help our partner acquire more education to progress in his or her career.

But none of us are invulnerable, and, in our role as caretaker, any of us may falter if we fail to pay proper attention to our own needs first.

Taking care of your own needs first may seem counterintuitive. It may even seem selfish. In fact, it is selfish. But I see nothing wrong in that. It is only by taking correct and consistent care of yourself that you can continue to fully support those you love.

Robert, an acquaintance of mine, had always helped his many friends, employees, and customers by sharing his time, advice, and money. He is widely considered to be extremely generous, and others constantly turned to him in their time of need. But, through no fault of his own, during the "Great Recession" of 2008 Robert lost half of his considerable net worth.

At lunch one day he confided in me. "Alan, I don't know what to do. If my business continues to decline the way it has during the past year or two I'm going to be in violation of loan agreements with my bank, run out of money, and my entire company could be lost to bankruptcy. But I don't want to abandon anyone."

"So you don't want to appear to be selfish," I said.

Robert corrected me. "I don't want to *be* selfish," he said.

"You're right." I sat and mused. "You seem to have a serious problem, and I don't have a ready answer for you. I'm going to have to think about this one."

The following week I invited Robert to early morning coffee at Starbucks.

"Is your business going any better?"

"I'm afraid not. If anything, my situation has gone from bad to worse in just this past week. And in ten days I will have to put a lot of new money into three separate projects. It will take every bit of my remaining business cash, and I'll have to get an equity loan on my home."

"Your home, Robert? What if you don't?"

"My company has been working on each of these projects for nearly two years. If I don't put in more money now, they will all have to be abandoned."

"Robert, I repeat. What if you don't?"

"Then I will have lost an investment of millions of dollars for myself and my investors, and we'll lose a great profit opportunity in the future. Even worse, I would have to lay off ten or twelve of my best people. Some of them have been with me for ten or fifteen years. How will they provide for their families?"

"Robert, you have to save yourself first."

"Alan, I want to. Believe me, I want to." He seemed near tears. "I've never had to let people go before."

I put my hand on his shoulder.

"Robert, I truly sympathize. If I had the money I would give it to you in a minute. But these are tough times for all of us, and if you don't take care of yourself first you may not be in a position to take care of anyone for years to come. It's like what you hear as part of the safety instructions before every airplane flight."

He looked at me curiously. Then he nodded his understanding.

"Put on your own oxygen mask first," he said.

"Robert, you got it. Exactly."

We hugged when we left the coffee shop.

I'm happy to report that Robert found enough money to fund the most important, and largest, of his three projects. One of his employees took early retirement, after admitting to Robert that she had always wanted to travel around the world. Other employees accepted a reduced salary in return for a share in the new venture they were working on.

Today that project is the most successful division in Robert's business, and two more of his now former employees are traveling the world in comfort.

To help others you must first protect your own well-being—emotionally and financially.

In a relationship with a romantic partner this also means that you cannot always meet his or her needs at the expense of your own. At times you absolutely must give yourself priority.

When my mother was dying, my father was her caretaker at home twenty-four hours a day. After nearly two months he hired a companion to be with Mom eight hours a day, six days a week.

"I just couldn't take it anymore," he said. "I had to get out of the house. I can now go to the park every day for a few hours and smoke a cigar."

"Dad, you don't have to persuade me. I'm glad that you have some help. Now you can take better care of Mom when you're with her."

If you need your own quiet time to read a book, take a walk or a yoga class, or have lunch with a friend, go for it. As I understand it, the essence of Buddhism is compassion, notably having compassion for yourself.

To paraphrase a quote attributed to Abraham Lincoln: You can help some of the people all of the time, all of the people some of the time, but you cannot help all of the people all of the time.

You have to take proper care of yourself and, when the need arises, put on your own oxygen mask first.

THE BEST DEFENSE
IS NO DEFENSE

A man should never be ashamed to own he has been in the wrong, which is but saying, in other words, that he is wiser today than he was yesterday.

—ALEXANDER POPE
"Thoughts On Various Subjects," *Miscellanies*, Volume 2

Several excuses are always less convincing than one.

—ALDOUS HUXLEY
Point Counter Point

When I think of defense I think of the 19th century American West, where pioneers huddled in forts protected from attack by walls and the US Army. I think of a castle in England, with drawbridge, gate, and moat. I think of Neighborhood Watch groups, trying to spot potential intruders and keep them out of the neighborhood. Defense, by definition, is designed to keep others away or chase them off.

But defense, while great on the battlefield or the sports arena, isn't always the best tactic in relationships.

In their excellent book *Do I Have to Give Up Me to Be Loved by You?* Jordan and Margaret Paul suggest a skill that I highly recommend, and, at times, even use myself.

When someone at work or at home has a problem with me (which, of course, is almost never ☺), I can respond with either "an intent to learn," or "an intent to defend." I can cower in my castle, shooting arrows and pouring boiling oil to keep the invader out; or I can roll down the drawbridge, open up my heavy gates, and invite the trespasser in for dinner.

Which would you prefer? Suppose you have invited me to dinner, and I am an hour late, with no explanation or apology. After a few moments of strained pleasantries, you might say, "Alan, you were an hour late. I was concerned."

I might offer several defenses:

"I wasn't late. This is the time you invited me for."

Or, "You know I'm usually late. You should have expected it."

Or, "The last two times I invited you to dinner you were half-an-hour late, so I didn't think timing mattered to you."

Or, "So what? Since when is being late a big deal?"

My possible defenses are infinite, and all of them are not just defensive, they are offensive. In so many words, I can tell you that I did nothing to offend you and suggest that, somehow, you are at fault.

If I do this, will you invite me back to dinner again anytime soon? I wouldn't invite you again if this happened to me—not because you were tardy, but because you were defensive. I wouldn't feel that you heard me, and, more importantly, I would fear that you might do the same thing again. I might even be downright angry with you. And if we were in a long-term relationship, my defensive behavior would, over time, erode all of your warm feelings toward me.

But suppose that instead of defending myself I expressed an intention to learn something and said, "Please say more."

You might then respond, "I spent hours preparing a special dinner, which has now been in the oven too long and is dry. I was also worried that you had been in an accident or that something horrible had happened to you."

And I could say, "Thanks for telling me. I have no excuse; I appreciate your invitation, and if you were an hour late, I would be concerned and feel the same way you do. If I am ever late again I promise to call you as soon as I realize there is a problem. My behavior is inexcusable, and I'm sorry."

This approach is much more likely to inspire a pleasant response, such as, "Thanks. I feel better now. Let's sit down together and enjoy dinner."

If you value friendships and intimacy, I suggest that the best defense is no defense at all. I invite you to permanently demolish the walls of your fortress, swing your castle gates wide open, ask those who are close to you how you can help them, and then invite them in.

"YES" IS THE BEST WORD

To say yes, you have to sweat and roll up your sleeves
and plunge both hands into life up to the elbows.

—JEAN ANOUILH
Antigone

"Nothing great was ever achieved without enthusiasm."

—RALPH WALDO EMERSON
"Circles," *Essays* (1841)

We all like to hear the word "yes." In fact, "yes" is one of those words that inspires me to wax poetic. Yes opens doors. Yes allows you to feel heard. Yes is the remedy for a long day filled with "no."

When it comes to relationships, the most important "yes" of all is an emotional one—especially if it's unconditional.

At home we all want intimacy and emotional support. After years of being happily married, I realize that I have not, and will not, get everything I want in my relationship. But I do know that the one thing I can count on is an unconditional, heartfelt "yes." This yes tells me that in spite of my flaws, Daveen approves of me and cares enough to let me know it without reservation.

Over time, any of us may become less attentive to the needs of our partner. That's human nature. Bestowing a full "yes" upon our partner's furrowed brow may not seem as important as it once did. But I am here to encourage you to remember the significance and power of saying "yes" to your partner.

But when is yes not really a yes? When it's a wishy-washy no disguised as a yes.

When you want to say "no," just say it. But on as many occasions as you can, give your partner the gift of an absolute "yes." It will feel wonderful for both of you.

And when you want to say "yes" to your partner, try not to say any of the following:

"I'll think about it."

"You want me to do what?"

"Thursday. Hmmm. That sounds nice."

"You asked for that before."

"Wait until after you have heard about my day."

"Houston, we have a problem." (This may be funny, but it's far from an embrace.)

"The children are . . . "

"The bathtub is . . . "

Or give "no" as the answer, because you aren't listening or are not paying attention.

These reactions are likely to make even the most enthusiastic partner feel more alone than before. When you reach out and receive a lukewarm response, in your heart you are going to feel rebuffed, unheard, and uncared for.

So, whenever possible, give your partner the best answer of all, a big enthusiastic "Yes."

For example, suppose I say to my wife, "Darling, I'd like to hug you." Then she responds, "Can't you see I'm cooking?" or "I'm taking the clothes out of the dryer."

You can see how these reactions might not feel good to someone who is clearly asking for and needing your attention.

Even, "Sure. I'd like to do that," won't feel nearly as good as a genuine, resounding, "Yes."

I have known one couple for more than forty years. The husband is one of my closest friends. I attended their wedding. My friend told me that early in their marriage his wife asked him, "Darling, would you do anything for me?"

"Yes," he answered. There was no hesitation, no holding back.

The next morning they talked about it. She said, "Last night you said 'yes' when I asked you if you would do anything for me."

"Yes."

"But you and I both know that you wouldn't. What if I asked you to quit your job, or move in with my parents, or do something you didn't feel good about morally? You wouldn't do it, would you?"

"I might do it. But that's not important. I know that you will seldom ask me to do anything I really don't want to do. And if you did, I would seriously consider how I could say 'yes' to you. And if I couldn't, I would answer you with appropriate reasons and trust that you would be okay with that."

"Then why did you say 'yes' so quickly last night?"

"Because I know you always go out of your way to be thoughtful about my feelings and concerns. I see that every day. I appreciate it, and I intend, for the rest our lives, to do whatever I can to help you to find the joy that you have brought to me. And that means I expect to say 'yes' as often and as sincerely as I can. It also means that when I say 'no,' I believe you will understand and respect my reasons."

"You do? Really?"

"Yes."

Recently I attended the celebration of their thirty-seventh wedding anniversary. This couple has lived the dream. Their children are now out of the house, they are together every night, and they travel often. Years ago they settled in, and then they settled for . . . not everything . . . but for something rather stunning. They are one of the happiest couples I have known.

Do I believe this?

Yes.

As Confucius says, "Wherever you go, go with all your heart."

PEOPLE TOOL
FOR LOVE & RELATIONSHIPS
18

THE FIVE KINDS OF "I'M SORRY"

To err is human; to forgive, divine.

—ALEXANDER POPE
"An Essay On Criticism"

True reconciliation does not consist in merely forgetting the past.

—NELSON MANDELA
Speech, January 7, 1996

Many people never say "I'm sorry." I'm sorry for them because they are going to repeatedly offend people in the same way. I'm sorry for the people they offend because it is going to happen again and again. This dynamic is extremely damaging for relationships.

When my wife Daveen and I arrived home late one Saturday evening after a full day—a play in the afternoon, dinner with friends, then a musical comedy in the evening—she said, "You seem distant. Does that have anything to do with me?"

"Yes, it does."

"What?"

"At dinner, you contradicted what I said in front of our company, without any particular reason. When you do this I am very uncomfortable and upset."

Daveen knew that I was right, and like so many of us in a similar situation was faced with a tough decision about how to respond. I'll tell you what she did, but first I'll list the five different kinds of "I'm sorry" she had to choose from, in ascending order of sincerity. The most effective is number five.

1. "I'm sorry you chose to respond so badly to what I did (or said)." This is not really an "I'm sorry" at all. It says that you think I was the one at fault because I responded badly.

2. "I'm sorry you're upset." This is a little better. It acknowledges that you have some regret. But it might also mean that you're unhappy with me because I'm upset with you. This one is more defensive than apologetic, especially when it is followed with the word "but."

3. "I'm sorry I said (or did) that." Now we're starting to cook. You have given an apology about your own words or action. You're not quite acknowledging your role in my unpleasant experience, but it is a good start.

4. "I'm sorry I hurt your feelings." We're almost there. You are acknowledging the cause and effect of the situation. You agree that you did something and that I reacted with hurt feelings. I can begin to heal. But I won't go all the way toward reconnecting with you because your "sorry" is still limited.

5. "I'm sorry." Eureka! We have found it! Simple, clear, and direct. You are telling me that you feel bad that I feel bad. My hardness toward you melts. I say, "Thank you," we reconnect, and we go on. A bonus that you might consider is, "I'm very sorry." Or, "I'm so sorry. I won't do that again." This one feels really good.

In any "us" situation it's important to say, "I'm sorry," and the exact way you say it is significant. If you want to establish or maintain trust and connection you need to quickly repair a relationship rupture.

When I'm offended, our bond is either stretched or severed, but if you sincerely and quickly apologize I feel my heart relax and I can more easily forgive you and forget the insult I felt.

Which one did Daveen use this evening? The best one, of course. She said, "I'm sorry. Thank you for telling me." Had she used one of the others, I probably would have responded in a way that would have hurt her feelings and—horror of horrors—I might have been called upon to say "I'm sorry" myself.

Silence, defensiveness, and recrimination are easy—and destructive. It takes thought, attention, and caring to preserve trust and to remain connected with a sincere, immediate, and simple "I'm sorry."

CATCH THEM BEING BETTER

Unsung, the noblest deed will die.

—PINDAR

A verse fragment from *Isthmian Odes*, IV

Good words are worth much, and cost little.

—GEORGE HERBERT

Jacula Prudentum, Proverb 155

If you want your children, or others, to repeat behavior that you like, try to "Catch Them Being Good" (as opposed to correcting them when they perform conduct you don't like). By praising performance, you encourage others to repeat it. This is the subject of a chapter in my first book, *People Tools*.

But your partner in life is not your child, a friend, or a coworker. Your partner in life is unique and should receive special attention. Sometimes, however, that "special attention" may be critical, caustic, or cutting.

For example, if your seven-year-old son or daughter is having trouble with spelling in school and proudly comes home one day with a perfect score on a spelling test, you are likely to say, "That's great! Good for you. I knew you could do it." Then everyone celebrates with high fives all around.

Suppose, however, your partner returns from the grocery store and proudly tells you, "Darling, this time I remembered everything.

I even found that special cheese which you've been asking for since last month."

Will it be high fives all around? Or might you respond, as I used to, with, "It's about time." Or perhaps with a sarcastic, "Finally!"

You may be frustrated with your partner's repeated failure to perform up to your standards. If you are, join the club. We all are irritated with our partners from time to time. Of course, your partner may be just as frustrated with you for your failure to live up to his or her expectations. Frustration is normal, especially with those we love and live with. You may have been equally frustrated with your seven-year-old's poor spelling. But would you even consider reacting to his or her first perfect spelling score with, "You've been so stupid on every other spelling test, you'll probably never get a decent score again"?

I cannot even imagine a parent ever saying words like that in response to their child's excitement and success. But we often speak to our partners using comments or reproaches we would never use with our children.

We might respond in ways that are funny and sarcastic, but also hurtful, especially when our partner shares excitement and success.

I have no objection to my wife, or anyone else, being funny. In fact, humor is often the best lubricant for friction in any human relationship. But if the joke is at your partner's expense, or includes the poison pill of blame, it is going to weaken your relationship, even if everyone laughs.

It's clear to me that your seven-year-old will respond to your praise by working just as hard, or harder, to master the words on next week's spelling test. By the same token if you want to encourage your partner to act in certain ways, start by making it okay for her or him to change. If you always remind them of past failures they are unlikely to even try to please you in the future.

When they're good, Catch Them Being Good. When they've transformed themselves from exasperating to exceptional, Catch Them Being Better.

If you want that special cheese, or special anything else, you had better make sure you express appropriate gratitude and praise for improvement. Otherwise, next time you may have to stop by the grocery store on your way home and buy that cheese for yourself. In fact, one day your partner may be bringing groceries home for someone else.

TAKE CARE
OF ONE ANOTHER

*Reverence for parents stands written among the three laws of
most revered righteousness.*

—Aeschylus
The Suppliants

*Mutual caring relationships require kindness and patience, toler-
ance, optimism, joy in the other's achievements, confidence in
oneself, and the ability to give without undue thought of gain.*

—Fred Rogers
*The World According to Mister Rogers:
Important Things to Remember*

When you share a life with someone, it is important to take care
of one another, and that includes taking care of those who are a part
of each other's lives. Daveen cares about my father, and we share
equally in our desire to take care of him. This not only enriches his
life, but our relationship as a couple as well.

My dad is one hundred years old and lives by himself in a house
that I built for him twelve years ago. He drives across town three
times a week to participate in his lawn bowling club. Dad likes to go
to the movies, so Daveen and I often invite him to join us.

Several months ago the three of us attended a movie at our favorite theater. From the parking garage we took several escalators up

to the theater. I asked my dad if he could climb one flight of stairs instead of taking the final escalator.

"Sure," he said. "I can do that."

Dad, Daveen, and I climbed the stairs and entered the theater. My dad needed to use the rest room before the movie started, so I waited for him outside.

I was sitting on a bench when two young men came out of the rest room calling my name. "Alan. Alan."

I stood up. "I'm Alan."

They ushered me into the men's bathroom. There was my dad, lying on the cold tile floor, with a cut on his face.

"What happened?"

"He fell. We called the paramedics."

"Dad, what happened?"

"I fell."

"Any broken bones?"

"No. But my shoulder hurts." I was alarmed to see that there was dried blood on his face.

Fifteen minutes later the paramedics arrived and trundled my dad into an ambulance. I rode with him, sirens blaring. Daveen drove our car to the hospital emergency room.

Thankfully, Dad was not seriously hurt. After reading his x-rays the emergency room doctor dressed his wounds, put his arm in a sling, and gave us a prescription for pain medication.

We drove Dad home. We never did see the movie.

On the way home Dad said, "I shouldn't have climbed the stairs. At the top, my legs were shaking. That's why I fell in the bathroom. I was having trouble standing up."

I was frustrated. But even though we hadn't seen the movie, and wouldn't get home until well after midnight, this was not the time for me to complain or launch into a lecture about "Why didn't you say something at the time." Not now. Not ever.

"Well, Dad, next time we'll all take the escalator to the top. No stairs."

"That would be a very good idea."

I like to make plans. I like to move fast. But my dad walks more slowly than I do. He usually links his arm with mine to protect us both against a fall. I need to allow extra time. And even though I like to climb the last flight of stairs to get a little exercise, now when I am with my father, we take the escalator.

Neither Daveen nor I gave it a second thought when we left the theater to take care of my dad after he fell. You would do the same.

And this Tool "Take Care of One Another" can apply to everyone, even strangers. At times it might even transcend the discipline of military orders.

At the conclusion of the film *A Few Good Men*, starring Tom Cruise as Lt. Daniel Kaffee and Jack Nicholson as Col. Nathan R. Jessup, the two Marines who followed Jack Nicholson's "Code Red" order are dishonorably discharged. Their final dialogue is:

> **Downey:** I don't understand . . . Colonel Jessup said he ordered the Code Red.
>
> **Galloway:** I know, but . . .
>
> **Downey:** Colonel Jessup said he ordered the Code Red! What did we do wrong?
>
> **Galloway:** It's not that simple . . .
>
> **Downey:** What did we do wrong? We did nothing wrong!
>
> **Dawson:** Yeah, we did. We were supposed to fight for people who couldn't fight for themselves. We were supposed to fight for Willy.

The lesson here is simple and fundamental.

Take care of one another. There is no other acceptable alternative.

PEOPLE TOOL
21
FOR LOVE & RELATIONSHIPS

CUDDLES

I want to do with you what spring does with the cherry trees.

—PABLO NERUDA
"Every Day You Play"
Twenty Love Poems and a Song of Despair

Those pleasures so lightly called physical.

—COLETTE (SIDONIE GABRIELLE COLETTE)
Mélanges

"Cuddles" should not just be the name of your granddaughter's new puppy. She, or he, is you and me.

Skin to skin contact is important for every human being. A great deal of research has indicated that infants who lack enough physical touch may never achieve full emotional development.

A study published by the National Academy of Sciences reports, "Children who have been deprived of close physical contact have lower levels of social-bonding hormones . . . Early cuddling is vital to a child's emotional well-being. Infants cared for by volunteer cuddlers may demonstrate greater growth, physiologic stability and have shorter hospital stays than babies without cuddling."

Maybe part of me is still a baby, but as a member of an adult couple, I find physical contact to be essential. It reinforces the connection between me and my partner, and it always provides comfort.

Occasionally I even tell Daveen that I need to cling to her for no particular reason. And she has always been available, without question or hesitation.

I also enjoy physical contact while walking. I'm pleased every time my father, now one hundred years old, interlocks his arm with mine as we walk together toward a restaurant, or to my car. After almost thirty-five years I am thrilled when Daveen reaches her arm around my waist as, for example, when we admire a particularly beautiful sunset.

Of course, our need for physical contact goes far beyond the sidewalk, and all the way into the bedroom. I'm not talking about sex here. I'm talking about physical contact and, in this case, cuddling.

Whether we have made love or not, whether we're tired or not, Daveen and I have cultivated the habit of cuddling as we lie in bed each night before we fall asleep. One of my favorite pleasures is when she falls asleep in my arms, breath slowing, her body relaxing into mine. I feel that Daveen trusts me with herself, which speaks to the very essence of our marriage, of "us."

Too often in our culture we are reluctant to hug, especially in public. Hugging between two men, or a man and a woman who are not romantically involved, can be seen as awkward because we fear, incorrectly, or assume, incorrectly, that a sexual component is involved. But, to paraphrase Freud, "a hug is just a hug."

The Peerless Quartet recorded a song more than one hundred years ago, yet you may remember it. Here is the refrain. You might try inserting "Cuddles" for "Sweetheart." I often do.

> Let me call you "Sweetheart," I'm in love with you.
> Let me hear you whisper that you love me too.
> Keep the love-light glowing in your eyes so true.
> Let me call you "Sweetheart," I'm in love with you.

Each of us spends enough time alone each day. Let's begin our day, or end it, with a cuddle or a hug.

ANGER IS A LONELY JOB

Anger is a short madness.
—HORACE (QUINTUS HORATIUS FLACCUS)
The Epistles, Book I

I was angry with my friend;
I told my wrath, my wrath did end.
I was angry with my foe;
I told it not, my wrath did grow.
—WILLIAM BLAKE
"A Poison Tree," *Songs of Experience* (1794)

I used to weigh 1,278 pounds—and one thousand pounds of that was anger.

Before our wedding, almost thirty-five years ago, I had the following conversation with Daveen.

"I have a bad habit," I said.

"Okay. What is it?"

"For some reason I have the idea that if I'm angry enough for long enough you will give me what I want."

"Yes, I have noticed that from time to time."

"I didn't think it would be a total surprise. But being angry is no fun. It colors the world rotten. And it's painful. I think what is really going on with me is that I believe that if I hurt deep enough and long enough I will get what I want, which seems absurd even to me."

"That doesn't make much sense to me either," she said.

"I agree. But that's how I feel."

"So what should I do about it?"

"Simply do this. When I'm grim and withdrawn, just say, 'Alan, you seem upset. If there is any way I can help right now, please let me know.'"

"Fine. I can do that. Then what?"

"Then leave me alone. When I'm angry I feel justified, I want to stay angry until I get satisfaction of some kind, but as much as I would like to, I have never stayed angry for more than three days. But don't buy into it. You might check back with me every four hours."

"Four hours it is!"

"Thanks . . ."

I now weigh two hundred and ten pounds. Over the years I have shed sixty-eight pounds of body weight and one thousand pounds of anger. To lose the anger, I used the same rule I use for worrying—if I can do something constructive about it now, then I do it. If not, I just let it go.

The truth is that my anger harms me much more than anyone else. But, in a way, it also feels wonderful. When I'm angry I feel wronged. I feel justified. I also feel clear and certain. Of course, it also feels nice to gulp down three desserts or two helpings of mashed potatoes. But there are costs, both to body and mind. And neither being angry nor overeating feels good later.

That's why, in the long run, it's better to lose those extra pounds of anger. My father has his own theory about this. He says that he refuses to send messages of stress to his body below his neck. This approach works well for Dad. He's in a good mood almost all of the time and is close to celebrating his next birthday when he will be one hundred and one years old. I think Dad is on to something. And for the rest of us, when we are burdened by all those pounds of extra anger, I suggest that you try what I have finally learned to do after all these years—let it go.

Anger is a lonely job. Fortunately, no one has to do it.

TAKE RESPONSIBILITY

Responsibility, n. A detachable burden easily shifted.

—AMBROSE BIERCE
The Devil's Dictionary

Very sorry can't come. Lie follows post.

—LORD CHARLES BERESFORD (1846–1919)
A telegraphed message to the Prince of Wales,
on being summoned to dine at the eleventh hour

The other day I was hurrying along the sidewalk on my way to a haircut when someone almost knocked me over. After regaining my balance, I turned to see the woman who had collided with me. Her dry cleaning was strewn around her on the cement pavement.

"I'm so sorry," she said. "The plastic wrap got caught in the door as I was leaving the cleaners and I tripped. I hope you aren't hurt."

"Not at all," I said. "I'm glad you're not hurt, yourself."

I helped her to pick up her dry cleaning. We smiled, she mumbled her apologies and thanks, and we continued on our separate ways.

As Chick Hearn, who broadcast 3,338 consecutive basketball games for the Los Angeles Lakers, would say, "No harm, no foul."

It is human nature to forgive an action that did not seem to be intentional. In this case it was obvious that the woman did not intend to run into me. Even though I was startled and almost fell down, I was not offended as soon as I realized it was an accident. If I believed she had bumped into me on purpose I would have reacted very differently. I might have glared at her or threatened to call my attorney.

We often apply a test of intent to the actions of others. We ask ourselves, "Was it intentional?" If something was annoying or hurtful, and we believe the act was deliberate, we might then become quite angry. If we believe the action was accidental and it was not truly hurtful, we are quick to pardon the potential offender.

In a relationship this lack of "intent" can sometimes be used as an excuse for insensitive behavior. This is especially true when this excuse is offered as a substitute for performance or being considerate. "I didn't mean to hurt your feelings," is often said instead of choosing not to say something insensitive in the first place. But when someone could choose to behave differently, and yet doesn't, their "intent" is suspect. And when this rationale is used too often it can damage the relationship.

My friend Joanna has been married to Hector for ten years. Joanna is a CPA. She prepares a household budget, pays her bills on time, and every year sets aside a portion of her income for retirement. Hector is a contractor who is often short of money.

When they married, Joanna owned her own home. Hector moved in with her, and at that time they agreed that Joanna would continue making the mortgage payments and Hector would pay half of the property taxes.

When the first property tax payment was due, Hector had a "business emergency" and said that he would pay his share "in a few weeks." This explanation was followed by, "I lost money on the job I was working on," "I had to catch up on payments to my ex-wife," and "My kids needed money for school supplies." According to Hector, he always had the intent to reimburse Joanna for his share, but somehow . . .

After three years of paying the full property tax herself, Joanna didn't ask him anymore.

My friend Gina is fond of the "I lost track of time" justification whenever she is late, which is often.

My friends don't loan me books anymore. I never intend to lose their books, but in the past forty years I don't remember returning a single one.

In each of these situations someone is abusing the test of "Intent." They are using their supposed lack of intent to evade responsibility for their behavior. It is always better to take responsibility for your words and actions. Don't allow "I didn't intend to" become your mantra, a misleading alibi for your failure to perform. You want your words to have integrity.

There will be times when you truly do not intend for something to happen. I suggest that you save that reason for the times you really are innocent of any blame. Nonstop justifications can prevent you from maintaining mutual trust. Excuses, after all, can get really old.

I did mean to make this a better chapter, but my publisher had me on a deadline and I ran out of time. Also, I saved my best ideas on a thumb drive. Unfortunately, my dog ate it.

PEOPLE TOOL
24
FOR LOVE & RELATIONSHIPS

LET'S TALK ABOUT MONEY

Money talks.
—APHRA BEHN
The Rover (1681)

Money doesn't talk, it screams.
—BOB DYLAN
"It's Alright Ma (I'm Only Bleeding)"

Talking about money is a strict taboo for many of us. We will talk about politics, parenting, current events, the weather, and even sex. But for some reason the subject of *money* is hidden in the safe deposit box of unspeakable topics, even between close family members.

One morning my second wife Susan brought up her parents' economic situation. She nervously cleared her throat and said, "I think my parents need financial help."

"Why do you think so?"

"I don't know," she shrugged. "It's a feeling I have."

"Okay. How much does your dad earn?"

"I don't know."

"Do you know how much money your parents have in the bank?"

"No."

"Do they have any big debts?"

"I suppose they owe something on their house."

"Have you talked to them about this?"

"No. Maybe you could."

I did. Susan's parents did not go into detail, but they did say that their finances were adequate.

Most parents, including Susan's, do not talk about money with their children.

Why? When my friend Albert told me that his brother had been promoted at work, my first question was, "How much is he earning?" When another friend, Susie, announced that her parents had bought a new home, I immediately asked her, "How much did they pay?"

Many of us do not talk about money because our parents cloaked their own finances in secrecy. Often we are afraid to appear to be ignorant, or to violate our partner's privacy. We think it's not "polite" to discuss money. We don't talk to our children about money because we fear that they might blab to their friends in school. For whatever reason, many families keep money a greater secret than the fact that a great uncle Herman was a bank robber.

Unfortunately, this aversion to money talk can cause serious problems in our intimate relationships. I'll give you an example.

Glenda, a former employee of mine, arrived at work one day completely distraught.

"We can't buy the house," she said.

"Why not? I thought that you and your husband love the house, and that everything was going well."

"We do love the house, but we can't buy it. I found out last night that Bob has terrible credit from before we were married. We can't qualify for a loan." Glenda began to cry.

I was surprised, but perhaps I shouldn't have been. Many couples simply do not talk about their finances, much less each other's credit scores, before they get married. Glenda eventually overcame her disappointment, in part because she ultimately married a new husband.

Fortunately for me, my parents talked to me about money freely, and I was a good listener. I knew how much my father earned as a studio musician (ten dollars an hour) and how many hours the union allowed him to work each week (ten). He told me how much cash flow he cleared from his two apartment buildings, and I soon figured out that his income amounted to one dollar and thirty-four cents an hour, twenty-four hours a day. This was at a time when, at my first job, I was earning the minimum wage of one dollar an hour. My father earned more money before he woke up in the morning than I earned by working all day.

Not only did my parents' openness about money teach me valuable business lessons that have benefited me throughout my life and career, they also set an example for how important financial transparency can be to healthy relationships and marriages.

And this transparency has helped me to be completely comfortable talking about money. I once asked a woman I just met how much she earned at her new job.

"I wouldn't even tell my mother that," she said.

"I won't tell your mother either."

She revealed her salary.

Why did she refuse to tell me at first? Because she was like so many people, uncomfortable talking about the subject of money. I imagine that her family never discussed it, just as my family never talked about sex.

Why then, after my brief attempt at humor, did she ultimately tell me? Because she realized that I was comfortable talking about money, even if she wasn't.

Today, information about money is easily accessible. You can research the cost of almost everything by looking it up on the Internet. You can learn the prices of houses, electronic devices, or automobiles. You can quickly discover salary ranges for your type of job in any location. You can determine the cost of living in every city in the United States. But even though information about money is readily available, talking about money still isn't.

I think you will agree that, like health, money is very important in your life. If I told you that I was suffering from a physical ailment, and yet I wouldn't tell you or anyone else what was wrong, you might accurately conclude that I wasn't going to get much help for my problem.

The same is true about money. You might be uncomfortable talking about it. You might be embarrassed or scared. If you are, I encourage you to seek the counsel of someone who is comfortable with the subject, and then start practicing. If you are more comfortable, you might start by discussing small amounts. Whether you're talking about one dollar or one million dollars, the principle is the same.

You may find that openness and honestly in the realm of money will bring deeper intimacy to your entire relationship. Both of you have to know about your financial capabilities and objectives, even if you plan to keep bank accounts completely separate.

We all know that "money talks." You and your partner, and your entire family, will profit by joining in that conversation.

NOW, NOT LATER

And all my days are trances,
And all my nightly dreams
Are where thy gray eye glances,
And where thy footstep gleams—
In what ethereal dances,
By what eternal streams.
—EDGAR ALLAN POE
"To One in Paradise"

Procrastination is the thief of time.
—WILLIAM SHAKESPEARE
The Two Gentleman of Verona

Now or later? Isn't that always the unavoidable question? These are the only two choices you have. What will you choose to do now, and what will you put off for later? Or put off until never?

If you are like me, there are some actions you take immediately and others you consistently postpone. I moved into my home four decades ago and have never once peeked inside a number of boxes that still sit in my garage containing who-knows-what. I suppose that one day my children may become the archeologists of my life.

On the other hand, there are many activities I never put off. I like to give and receive hugs. This is one activity I perform personally, immediately, and enthusiastically. I am also a fanatic about paying my bills on time, as well as immediately collecting any money that is due to me.

In relationships we often focus on the major or most memorable events, such as my father's one-hundredth birthday party last year. We all look forward to, or back upon, weddings, a first kiss, or an unforgettable journey. A major part of our lives is spent harboring high hopes and cherishing fond memories.

But the most important milestones in any relationship—meeting for the first time, falling in love, meeting his or her parents—are rare. In fact, when you think about it, most of our days together are routine. We wake up, shower, eat breakfast, commute, run errands, share dinner, watch television or talk with friends, and then we fall asleep.

And all too often, in the humdrum hurry of our lives, we lose sight of the truth that relationships are created or destroyed by the small compassions or cruelties we visit upon each other in the here and now—minute by minute, hour by hour, day by day.

This is the reality upon which every successful long-term relationship is shaped and sustained. How do you relate to each other each day, especially when you encounter a difference of opinion or serious difficulty? The immediacy of now cannot be postponed until later. Now is the only time you have to build your relationships. Later is too late because later may mean never.

There are two important principals of "now." Everyone wants attention—now, not later. Your five-year-old wants your attention now, and doesn't care about your important telephone call or how the World Cup soccer game turns out. And every single one of us seeks a positive response. If you respond to your partner long after he or she has shared something important, your response will have lost its value. Try saying, "That is terrific!" the next day and they're going to give you a blank stare and wonder what you are talking about. Yesterday or a month ago, or whenever they gave you the news, is when saying "terrific" would have been, well, terrific.

This is why I am happy when my day begins with a smile and cheerful "Good morning" from Daveen or from one of my coworkers at my office. And I always like a "Glad to see you" when I arrive home. I am pleased when a friend gives me a gift for no special reason. You do not have to wait for "later" to send a card, give a gift, or text a friend those beautiful words "I've been thinking of you."

I spend a lot of time each day contemplating my computer screen. I receive more emails in a day than I can possibly answer, and I either respond immediately or, perhaps you guessed it, never.

I have two methods that help me to connect with those I choose to spend my time with in the here and now. First, I delegate as much as I possibly can (although this doesn't work with relationships). Second, I cut toxic people out of my life. Isn't that what the "delete" button is for?

With venomous people you can improve your life and your relationships radically by following the example of my father. To me this story is sad, but I do agree with Dad's conclusion. You have to remember that, in any relationship, you are living your life for yourself first. You can't allow others, no matter how close, constantly drag you into the darkness of their own angst.

My grandfather, Abraham Fox, lived to be ninety-four. For the last twenty years of his life he lived in Florida, while my family lived in California. My father used to correspond with him, but Abe never shared a kind word. My father finally wrote to my grandfather and said, "Let's write about pleasant memories in our letters and talk about our problems when we see each other."

Three weeks later Dad received his father's reply. "I don't remember a single happy time in our relationship."

Dad never saw or communicated with his father again. I feel sad in writing this, and I make a point to see my father regularly. But we both are always positive, about each other and our relationship.

When you have an encouraging thought or impulse, say it or do it. Thank a friend who invites you for dinner. Bake cookies for everyone at work. If you want to enjoy satisfying moments with others, take the initiative and start by sharing pleasant thoughts and moments with them . . . now, not later.

Compliments, consideration, and charm belong in your life now, and since yesterday is but a memory and tomorrow only a dream, there can no finer time than now for a smile, a hug, or a cheerful text message.

My good friend John was a journalist. At one time he worked with people who were nearing the end of their lives.

"Is there anything in your life which you regret?" he would ask.

"Alan," he said to me, "not one person, not one, has ever told me that they regretted something they had done. Their regret was always about what they hadn't done."

We only have today. Let's make the most of it. Now, not later.

TIME AND QUALITY

Time is the thing we least have of.
—EARNEST HEMMINGWAY
Quoted in *The New Yorker*, May 13, 1950

We haven't the time to take our time.
—EUGENE IONESCO
Exit the King

What is it that you really want from any relationship? For me the answer is clear and simple. I want two things: First, enough time together. Second, the highest possible quality of communication during that time.

How much time is enough? That depends on the nature of your relationship. Cathy is the general manager of my business. Cathy and I have worked together for more than thirty years. Cathy is usually in her office by ten and works into the evening. Cathy is seldom in her office on the weekend, although she takes her briefcase home and is available electronically.

This arrangement works perfectly for both of us. Although I frequently work outside the office on weekdays, and I'm often sitting at my office desk on weekends, Cathy and I connect on those days when we are in the office together. When we need to consult, we make ourselves available. In our long and productive relationship Cathy and

I have had only a few strong disagreements, which we settled in less than a day. I seldom contact Cathy on weekends other than by emails that she can answer at her leisure. I believe she is entitled to use her personal time as she sees fit. With Cathy, our limited time together is sufficient, because the quality of that time is so high.

The situation is different with my CFO, Ed, who has been with me almost as long as Cathy. Ed is more of a free spirit when it comes to where and when he works. Years ago I was upset with Ed because he would disappear from the office after lunch several days a week to care for his two young children when his wife's work schedule required.

The problem for me was that I needed to consult with Ed frequently and often found him missing. In this case timing was vital, because a financial opportunity can vanish in ten minutes. Since cell phones had just become available, Ed and I agreed that when he was outside the office Ed would make himself available by phone. I still remember his outstanding contribution to an hour-long conference call while he was fishing on Lake Tahoe.

It's not always easy to arrange quality time with your partner. My wife, Daveen, keeps extremely busy. She will occasionally leave the house before 6:00 a.m. to pick up a friend at the airport, and in the evening she often spends time on the phone, talking to one of our children or one of her many friends. For several years Daveen served as Head of School at an independent elementary and middle school, and she was more in demand than I was. During that time, we were so busy that we had to make appointments to see each other. Fortunately, the quality of our time together remained relatively high. But I don't believe that either of us was entirely satisfied with the amount of time we were able to spend together.

Today, Daveen and I have learned to build "us" time into our schedules. We have a standing date to be in our bedroom together at 9:00 p.m. on weekdays. No cell phones, no emails, no texting. It's just the two of us, chatting about our day. On weekends we generally travel or attend social functions, which we both enjoy. As partners, our time together is essential. To remain meaningfully connected we have to build this element into our lives so that each of us is satisfied.

A relationship is not a prison, but in order for your primary relationships to be successful, you do need to allocate sufficient time for each other. There is no standard formula, of course. It's up to each couple to decide the issue of how much time they spend together. I knew one couple, married for ten years, who preferred to only spend weekends with each other.

And since each of us can only be in one place at a time, it's important to give your partner the space to pursue her or his own interests when we're apart. Keep in touch electronically if you like. I hope that Daveen enjoys whatever she is doing when she is not with me, and that it will enhance the quality of our time together.

When we are together, we make it count.

Time and quality. These are the essence of every successful relationship.

PEOPLE TOOL
FOR LOVE & RELATIONSHIPS
27

THE FIELD OF BATTLE

'In my youth,' said his father, 'I took to the law
and argued each case with my wife;
And the muscular strength which it gave to my jaw,
Has lasted the rest of my life.'

—LEWIS CARROLL
Alice's Adventures in Wonderland

Know the enemy and know yourself;
in a hundred battles, you will never be defeated.

—SUN TZU
The Art of War (Translation by Yuan Shibang)

Every couple is composed of two different human beings. This means that differences of opinion are inevitable. Since each of us likes to be validated by the other, and because we also like to get what we want, there is often a battle as to which of two views will prevail.

For example, I like Daveen to be in bed at the same time I am, but sometimes she still has something else she has to do and joins me ten or fifteen minutes later. Neither of us is "right" or "wrong" in this situation; our timing is just different.

Daveen and I recently took a walking tour of the Bavarian town of Regensburg. Our guide was half Polish and half Norwegian. Her husband was German. She shared with us an interesting observation about their diverse points of view:

"Poles and Germans have fought many battles over the years. It's interesting to me that, in his understanding of this history, the great battles fought between Germany and Poland are those in which the Germans won. My outlook, of course, as taught to me in my schools, is that Poland won all the big battles."

Suppose that you and I are going to fight a duel. You are an expert with a sword. I am a marksman with a pistol. Who is more likely to "win" the dispute? The answer, of course, does not depend in any way on who has the better argument. The winner will almost certainly be the one who has the advantage on the field of battle. Swords? I am skewered. Pistols? You are going to be on the ground.

What does this have to do with differences—dare I say arguments—between partners? Everything. The partner who selects the field of battle has the advantage.

In the physical realm, this is obvious. If I am bigger, stronger, quicker, and more aggressive than you are I will have the advantage in a physical confrontation. If you have a greater vocabulary, verbal dexterity, and mental determination, you will have the advantage in a spoken dispute.

One common field of battle is the emotional. Here the winning strategy is caring less about the outcome than your partner (or should I say your adversary).

By "the winning strategy" I am not talking about who "wins" the actual argument. "Winning" the argument is the easy part. The mere words, "I don't understand why this is so important to you," repeated dozens or hundreds of times, will carry the day.

"I need to see my mail the day it comes in."

"I don't understand why this is so important to you."

"It has always been important to me."

"I don't understand why this is so important to you."

"Maybe it's because I like to pay my bills on time. Maybe I'll receive a check. Maybe I want to read junk mail."

"I don't understand why this is so important to you."

The "I don't understand" partner who sticks to his or her position is going to win the verbal argument every time. The dispute is not going to be resolved to the other's satisfaction.

My General Theory of Human Relativity is this: We have different needs and different points of view. We express our differences on diverse fields of battle in which one side must win. That means the other side must lose.

But in a partnership held together by an emotional bond, neither partner "wins" when the bond itself is diluted. When one partner repeatedly insists on his or her point of view the other partner may feel unheard, abandoned, or both. Who is the "winner"? No one—unless one partner wants a weaker emotional bond. This is why I maintain that the partner who cares less will impose his or her will. If winning the argument results in greater emotional distance, then it ultimately works to the advantage of the one who does not want to be as close.

What can you do if you are the partner who cares more? Choose an Intent to Learn in the Field of Battle, where there is no Judgment, no Winner, and no Loser. With Intent to Learn, the goal is merely to learn, empathize, and understand your partner's need or point of view.

Can there be a difference of opinion without a winner and a loser? Absolutely. If each partner demonstrates a determination to address the needs and differences of the other partner, I believe a "win-win" is likely.

Of course, part of me is now saying to myself, "What nonsense. In a dispute there has to be a winner, and when there is a winner there must also be a loser." But I'm not going to argue about that with myself, because when I argue with myself I always win. And I always lose. Just like a couple. Go figure. And the beat goes on.

APPEAL TO THEIR SELF-INTEREST

Cui bono?
("To whose profit?")
—CICERO
Pro Roscio Amerino, a speech given on behalf of Roscius Ameria

All sensible people are selfish, and nature is tugging
at every contract to make the terms of it fair.
—RALPH WALDO EMERSON
The Conduct of Life

I would like you to contact ten friends right now and insist that each of them buy five copies of this book.

Thank you.

Wait a minute. You haven't done it yet? Why in the world not? I'm a nice guy. My publisher is even nicer than I am. Bookstore owners are wonderful people, and your local bookstore is probably struggling to earn a profit. If your friends buy fifty of my books from them at full price, it will help independent bookstores to stay afloat.

Not yet convinced? Okay, I'll continue. I'm happier when I sell more books, and when I'm happier I'm nicer to my wife. When I'm nicer to my wife, she is nicer to me. Go ahead. Do it to please me or to please my wife. Do it because I want you to. But hurry up, because I'm running out of arguments.

All right. It seems like I'm talking to myself here. You're just reading along, scratching your head, and probably thinking that the one copy of my book you already have is enough. Maybe more than enough.

My sales pitch is obviously not working. And why do you think that is?

Duh! It's because I missed one fundamental point. I failed to effectively appeal to your self-interest. I was making it all about me (or my wife or your local bookstore) and not about you.

I've read a few books on salesmanship, and each of those books presents similar ideas: Know your customer. Find out what he or she wants. Give your customers value. Advertise. Praise the virtues of your product. Create a website and build an engaged community. And so on. There are many valid principles out there.

But true salesmanship boils down to one simple concept, which is this: Appeal to your customer's self-interest. If you remember just one suggestion from this entire book, please make it this one:

APPEAL TO YOUR CUSTOMER'S (OR PARTNER'S) SELF-INTEREST.

Why? Because learning and practicing that simple skill is all you need to know about persuading other people to do what you would like them to do. And this is extremely important in your close relationships, not just to get your way, but also to learn how to make your partner happier by fulfilling his or her needs.

There's a joke I love to tell at weddings. Just after the ceremony, when everyone is sharing a few words of wisdom and encouragement for the happy couple, I will often say, "Congratulations! Now that you're married you can kick off those tight shoes. You don't have to ever look your best again. You won!"

This is only funny, of course, because everyone who has ever been married knows it isn't true.

You may have spent years trying to impress your new spouse enough so she or he will marry you. But in order to truly live happily ever after, you will have to commit to "After-Sales Service" (discussed in *People Tools for Business*) for the rest of your life. You will still have to remain sensitive to each other's needs and desires. If not, your relationship may not endure for as long as you may have wished.

One of my favorite cartoons illustrates how partners sometimes come into a marriage with very different ideas. It shows a couple standing at the altar. He is thinking, "This is great. Now I get all the sex I want." She is thinking, "Thank goodness I don't have to do *that* anymore."

Eve, a good friend of mine who is also one of my original investors, met with me at my office last week to discuss her investments.

"Two of my properties aren't doing very well, and, as you know, I'm retired. I want you to buy back those two investments at the same price I paid, and put me into something else which will have a much higher cash flow."

Did that approach effectively appeal to my self-interest? Not exactly.

I often replace properties to provide a higher cash flow for an investor. But the flavor of Eve's request was that I should do it because she felt entitled. Her request seemed more like a demand. Of course, I always want to support my friends, so once I got over my initial surprise, I found a way to make us both happy.

Eventually, after the first glow of love has merged into reality, you and your partner are going to start asking yourselves the same thing: "What's in it for me?"

And if you expect to continue getting the best, the absolute best, from your partner, you're going to have to come up with some effective answers to this question. What do you offer them in exchange for all that they do for you? What are they going to get out of attending another boring business party with you? What is their reward for working seventy hours a week to save money to take you on a vacation? Why should she bake your favorite cake? Why should he shop for groceries or cook your dinner or take care of the children while you study for your master's degree?

"I love you—therefore you owe me half of your paycheck" is not going to work forever. Neither will, "You love me—therefore you should wash my car, clean the house, and take our three dogs to the vet. And you should do this even though I disappear for weeks at a time to go fishing with my friends."

As they say about sarcasm, "Sure. That'll work."

Your partner does not owe you anything, except to work with you to make both of your lives together the best they can possibly be. And, to prosper, every relationship must be perceived as approximately equal by both partners most of the time.

Your partner has just as much right to what he or she wants as you do.

Often when in bed at night, my wife asks me to scratch her back, and I am happy to fulfill her wish. That is, of course, on condition that she scratches my back in return.

Now, about those fifty books . . .

PEOPLE TOOL
FOR LOVE & RELATIONSHIPS
29

TIMING

There is a time for everything.
—GEOFFREY CHAUCER
The Canterbury Tales

To every thing there is a season,
and a time to every purpose under the heaven . . .
—ECCLESIATES 3:1-2

One of my favorite jokes goes like this: I ask you to ask me, "What is the most important part of telling a joke?" Sometimes I need to ask more than once because the person doesn't know I'm about to give a one-liner. So I'll ask you again to ask me, "What is the most important part of telling a . . . "

As you begin to ask, I interrupt you, saying, "TIMING! Ha ha."

Then you laugh because I disrupted your timing. Get it? Go ahead. I'll wait.

Sometimes I forget and let you ask the entire question, "What is the most important part of telling a joke?"

Then I say, "Timing."

That's not funny, unless you find humor in my telling a joke badly.

But timing doesn't just apply to jokes. Awareness of timing is an essential element in every thriving relationship.

One morning I was already deep into work in my office when Cathy, my general manager, arrived. Part of her job is to oversee accounting, and I had just discovered a major problem with our financial statements. I was upset.

Before she even put down her purse and briefcase I said, "Cathy, I've been looking through our monthly reports and there is a serious problem here. It seems that . . ."

"Alan," she said, "you've got to say 'hello' before you start hitting me with problems."

"I'm sorry, Cathy. Hello." I may have even smiled, weakly. Then I continued. "As I was saying, there is a serious problem with . . ."

From that day to this, when I assail Cathy with a problem in the morning, I often interrupt myself to ask her, "Have I said 'hello' to you yet today?"

Fortunately for both of us, Cathy laughs, because we both know that I already have said "hello" (I wouldn't dare not to), and this recurring parody of myself takes the edge off whatever the problem of the moment happens to be.

Sometimes in a relationship you need to wait for the right time to connect.

My C.P.A., Ray, has a long-standing habit. Before he leaves for work in the morning he switches to work mode. From that moment on it's not a good idea to ask him how he liked his breakfast or what he wants for dinner, because Ray is not thinking about those subjects. He's already thinking about balance sheets and the client he is about to meet.

Ray's wife, Ann, likes to walk him to his car. One morning, as Ray was opening the driver's door, she said, "I want to have a quiet moment of connection." Ann placed her hands on his shoulders and gazed fondly into his eyes. He gazed back, but at something on the wall behind her. He was already thinking about numbers.

As you might imagine, Ann's "moment of connection" didn't go fabulously well. Even after ten years of marriage Ann didn't recognize that Ray was not about to detach from his obsession with debits and credits. Consequently, he was not emotionally present for a semi-romantic moment. This is a classic case of imperfect timing.

Kids are impatient and aren't very good at waiting. There is a famous research project that I think of as "The Marshmallow Report." The researcher would put a marshmallow on the table in front of a young child and tell the child that he was going to leave the room for a few minutes. He would then say:

"If the marshmallow is on the table when I get back, I'll give you another marshmallow."

Naturally some of the children didn't wait and ate the marshmallow before the researcher returned. However, the interesting results of the long-term study showed that those children who did wait, performed better as teenagers on their college entrance exams. Timing, which often requires patience, is an important skill to cultivate in life, as well as in relationships.

But not all of us will wait for that second marshmallow. I'm impatient. I want what I want, and I want it yesterday. I have learned, however, that with Cathy and everyone else, I have a better relationship when I pay attention to their needs and say "hello" before getting into the business problem at hand. I'm willing to delay the satisfaction of my needs to a time when I will achieve a better result. I am, above all, a practicing pragmatist.

In my office my employees know that if they want something from me, their timing is important. I have occasionally said, "I know that your annual review is scheduled for this morning, but I'm in a bad mood today and think I can be more objective about your salary increase if we postpone your review until tomorrow." I'm happy to report that all of my employees are both bright and sensitive. When asked, every single one of them has been willing to wait. And they achieve a better result by paying attention to the matter of timing.

I think I've been more than patient here. Now I want to tell you one of my favorite jokes. Ask me, "What is the most important part of telling a . . . "

"TIMING!"

MIND READING—
IF YOU LOVED ME
I WOULDN'T HAVE TO ASK

Love is a joint experience between two persons—but the fact that it is a joint experience does not mean that it is a similar experience to the two people involved.

—CARSON MCCULLERS
The Ballad of the Sad Café

If a man will begin with certainties, he shall end in doubts; but if he will be content to begin with doubts he shall end in certainties.

—FRANCIS BACON
Meditationes Sacrae (1597)

I used to believe that if I had to ask you for something, and even if you then quickly gave it to me, our relationship must be without great value. I thought if you really cared for me you would provide whatever I needed without my having to go to the risk and trouble of asking you for it.

Just how logical is this idea? Let's give it a try. Take a few seconds, close your eyes, and then tell me what I want most right now. I'll count to ten while I wait for you to figure it out.

All right. Time's up. I want a glass of water. If you didn't read my mind correctly, shame on you. I can only conclude that you don't really care about me, and we are never going to have a close relationship.

Am I alone in this mind-reading belief? After all, it's so logical. My mother knew what I wanted. And sometimes she gave me what I wanted without my even having to tell her. My mother really loved me.

The problem with the mind-reading hypothesis is that no one since my mother has been very good at it, and sometimes I even had to give *her* a few hints. ("Mom, no more wool sweaters, please. They itch and I don't like to wear them.")

As you might imagine, I've found it much more effective to not leave communication to telepathy, but to express my desires clearly. I have discovered that the food at many restaurants is excellent when I state in advance exactly what I want and how I would like it to be cooked. In my business everyone I work with, including me, performs best when the goal, and the instructions, are clear. And at home I don't mind asking for what I want because asking significantly increases my chance of getting it.

I no longer take responsibility for my failure to read other people's minds because success with this is unreliable, if not impossible.

The State of California recently even revoked my license in mind reading because I scored so poorly on all of their mind-reading tests.

Years ago I gave up "surprising" my children with a birthday or Christmas present. That's because, time after time, they would tear off the wrapping paper, smile awkwardly, and say, "Wow, Dad. This is exactly what I wanted. How did you ever guess?" Now they just say, "This is exactly what I wanted," because my gift to them is cash. It's not a surprise, but it is a lot more effective than giving them another wool sweater.

At an annual review in my office I always ask my employees to tell me what new salary they expect, and why. I prefer to start from there, rather than guessing and being uncertain for an entire year whether they are really pleased or really disappointed.

In contract law there is a concept of a "meeting of the minds." You agree to build a house for me, and I agree to pay you a fixed amount of money. If I expect a ten-thousand-square-foot mansion, and you expected to provide a small wood shack in my back yard, there would be no "meeting of the minds," and there could be no enforceable contract because the material details of our supposed agreement are vastly different. There is a good reason for this, which is obvious when you think about it. That is why a building contract will have explicit specifications and provisions for change orders to be in writing if there are any modifications.

The bottom line is, if you want something, ask for it and be specific. No more mind reading. Don't expect your partner to know what you are thinking. That sets everyone up for failure. And let's just agree that I love you and you love me, even if we do have to tell each other out loud what it is we want. (Scratch my back a little more to the left. No, my left.)

Close your eyes for just a minute, and open your mind.

Ahhh. Thank you. I'm glad you liked this chapter and want to read it again.

MORE IS NOT
ALWAYS BETTER

It is quality rather than quantity that matters.
—LUCIUS ANNAEUS SENECA
Epistles, Volume 1, 45

You never know what is enough
unless you know what is more than enough.
—WILLIAM BLAKE
The Marriage of Heaven and Hell, Proverbs of Hell, 46

Have you ever walked out of a movie and said, "It was good, but I would have liked it better if it had been a few minutes shorter"? Have you ever wondered why TED talks are limited to twenty minutes? I'm sure you have noticed that the chapters of this book are no longer than four or five pages. There is a reason for this.

One year ago I was on a deadline to finish my second book, *People Tools for Business*. I called my son Craig, who is a professor at the Anderson School of Business at UCLA, and mentioned that I still had to write eight chapters to reach my goal.

"Don't do it," he said.

"What do you mean, 'Don't do it'? I promised myself I'd write this number and my publisher expects sixty chapters."

"Dad, you are the victim of 'The Presenter's Paradox'."

"All right, Craig. What's 'The Presenter's Paradox'?"

"Basically, it says that presenters believe the more information they include the better their presentation will be received."

"That makes sense to me."

Ever since he was a senior in college Craig has been fond of citing psychology studies. And he has always been exactly on target.

"Dad, the research shows that an audience evaluates material based upon its average quality, not based on its length."

"So you are saying that even if I did write the sixty chapters, I should take out the weakest ten and my book would be better received?"

"Exactly."

I'm always open to advice, especially when it saves me time and improves my work. I recalled the show business adage, "Leave 'em wanting more." (See the People Tool "Showbiz" in my first book, *People Tools*.)

How does this apply to love and relationships?

I know a woman, Betty, who is a professor at the Stanford Law School. She has enjoyed a ten-year relationship with Howard, who owns a large national business based in Phoenix. They fly to see each other every other weekend. Recently Betty told me they have grown extremely close over the past three years.

"Why?" I said.

"Because each time we're together is like a honeymoon. And while I would like Howard to move to Palo Alto so that we could see each other every day, I suspect that if we were together all of the time that might change. And not for the better."

Another friend of mine, John, used to spend one or two weeks every month traveling on business (before he retired). His wife, Leanne, used to attend ten-day meditation groups three or four times a year. And yet, in spite of spending a lot of time apart, they seemed devoted to each other. Maybe their temporary separations kept their marriage fresh.

As Kahlil Gibran writes in *The Prophet*:

> *Sing and dance together and be joyous,*
> *but let each one of you be alone,*
>
> *Even as the strings of a lute are alone*
> *though they quiver with the same music.*

Spending more time together is not always better. Take, for example, retired couples who often need to find separately their own independent activities to keep from getting on each other's nerves.

Perhaps Betty and Howard already have the best relationship possible for them. It's just human nature that when you spend time apart you look forward to and treasure your time together. More is not always better.

RELIABLE AND EXCITING

*We may affirm absolutely that nothing great in the world
has been accomplished without passion.*
—GEORG WILHELM FRIEDRICH HEGEL
Philosophy of History

*Fantasy is like jam. You have to spread it
on a solid piece of bread.*
—ITALO CALVINO
New York Review of Books, November 21, 1985

This past year I took a cruise down the Danube River on a brand new Viking River Cruises boat. For me this was an ideal vacation for two reasons:

1. It was reliable. I slept in the same bed every night. There was no need to check into different hotels. There was no pressure to search for new restaurants. I enjoyed my meals in the same dining room. I didn't have to pack and unpack, suffer through security at airports, or deal with unpredictable drivers. I experienced the reliability and comfort of the known. That's nice.

2. It was also exciting. I visited a different town each day. I stood on the small balcony and watched fresh scenery come into view. I was able to enjoy both the thrill of discovery and the excitement of variety. It was a perfect mixture.

I like the combination of reliable and exciting, in life and in my relationships. But how can you achieve both reliability and excitement in the same relationship, especially over many years?

I have several thoughts on this.

First, keep your relationship solid, and that begins and ends with mutual trust. Establishing trust in a relationship can be difficult, because we have to believe in another human being over whom we have no control. And none of us can be entirely predictable or reliable. A partner might get sick at an inconvenient time. You might run out of money when you both really need it. You might lie to avoid telling an important truth that your partner might dislike. And he or she might lie to you occasionally for similar reasons. And one big lie can damage your willingness to trust someone for many years, if not forever.

And yet, after almost thirty-five years of my present marriage, raising six children, and sleeping together in the same bed for more than twelve thousand nights (that's almost thirty-five years), I have always chosen to trust my partner's underlying good intentions.

I can trust that my partner will remain as committed to my well-being as I am to hers. And I suggest you do the same. Trust your partner as much as you can. You have to especially believe that he or she has your best interests at heart. Because if they don't, or if you truly think that they don't, then you should certainly consider not staying with them. (See the People Tool of "Abandon Ship.")

It's even more important to trust yourself. Trust that you will be able to remain loyal to your partner, and that the two of you can deal with difficult and unpredictable circumstances, such as sickness or financial problems, as they arise. Mutual trust is about as good as it gets in this life, both in business and personal relationships.

After establishing mutual trust, how is it possible to maintain excitement in a long-standing relationship?

First, rely on that foundation of trust to "let yourself go," and ask your partner to "let go" as well. Use your imagination in the bedroom and encourage your partner to do the same. Above all, stay positive.

"That sounds exciting," is far more appealing than "You want to do what!?" I always try to keep my first response positive.

"You want to make love while riding on an elephant? That is really creative." Of course, since I have vowed never to ride on an elephant again, my initial response would be followed by, "I would hate to get seasick on you. Would you consider an elephant poster on our bedroom wall?"

In other words, an expression of interest is not the same as approval or agreement, but it can make the ultimate "no" far more palatable.

Second, go for variety in your regular activities. Try a no-utensil dinner (maybe not with your children, but who knows.) Take your vacation somewhere new that you've always wanted to visit. Surf the Internet to discover groups or activities in which both of you have an interest.

With a foundation of trust, and a structure of openness and fantasy, you can keep any relationship both reliable and exciting. And in my book it doesn't get any better than that.

DISCONNECT

I have found you an argument. I am not
obliged to find you an understanding.

—SAMUEL JOHNSON
Boswell, *Life of Johnson*

An argument needs no reason, nor a friendship.

—IBYCUS
Poem Fragment 40, ca. 542 BCE

Whether you've been together for two years or twenty, you've probably had the same argument with your partner multiple times. Frustrating, isn't it? She or he is sooo . . . well, just so stubborn. Of course, that may be exactly what he or she is thinking about you. Horrors!

In these situations, I find the best solution is to "disconnect."

"Disconnect" means exactly what it says. Disconnect. Stop arguing. Stop talking about it, and change the subject if you can. Walk away, if you must. Do not have the same argument, which is going to yield the same result, for the fiftieth or sixtieth time.

Learning to "disconnect" is especially important during disagreements on your essential "core values" on which you will never compromise as discussed in chapter 7. We all have our own individual core values. For example, I will not live with a partner who engages in smoking, heavy drinking, or arguing in public. I also won't be with a partner who squanders money, who does not have my back, or who is critical or negative much of the time.

I'm not saying that any of these core values of mine should apply to you. Your list of core values is your own. Maybe you could never live with a person who won't attend social events with you, complains constantly about something but will never take action to change it, or who ignores you when he or she is focused on writing.

If either you or your partner, or potential partner, has a core issue on which you disagree ("he wants to have children, and I don't" or "she lives with six cats, and I'm terribly allergic to cat dander"), you simply have to disconnect and move on, without a backward glance. Your argument will never be resolved unless one of you changes his or her position. On a core issue that possibility is unlikely, and it is essential for your long-term happiness to discover those core values sooner rather than later. If not, you are doomed to spend years of your life arguing, while hoping that your partner will change. Of course, your partner is also hoping that you will change, and the two of you are going to end up with a stalemate. (Pun intended.)

If the argument is not about a core issue, then you are disagreeing about a preference, such as whether or not to attend a party together. A dispute over preferences is really just a power struggle in which even the winner loses. One or both of you could compromise. You might consider the system on ball possession in college basketball and take turns compromising. If you won't consider that, then I repeat—it's either a core issue that will never be resolved, or a power struggle in which there are two losers. Disconnect.

I've also heard it said that a definition of insanity is repeating the same action over and over again and expecting a different result.

Before Daveen and I were married, I told her that I knew it was important to her that I keep my part of our bedroom more neat than I was in the habit of doing. This was a reasonable request from her, but difficult for me to execute. It seemed to be a core-issue problem for each of us. We resolved it by the compromise of my being neater and Daveen helping out.

You do not have to recreate the Civil War every week or every month. Core values will remain and must be recognized and discussed early in your relationship. Preferences will have to be considered on a case-by-case basis, but to make your relationship work well each of you is going to have to compromise. Our Norwegian/Polish guide in Regensburg, Germany, spoke seven languages and was married to a German gentleman. She said, "We have agreed to always argue in English, because if we argue in German he always wins."

When headed down that same discordant road for the umpteenth time, disconnect— not with anger or disapproval, but simply to take care of yourself and your relationship. The first time may be scary, but you will succeed if you persevere. And, of course, later, you should not be hesitant to reconnect.

Try it. You might both like it.

PUT IT IN WRITING

God is Love, but get it in writing.
—GYPSY ROSE LEE
Quoted in *The New York Times*, December 1, 1988

A verbal contract isn't worth the paper it's written on.
—SAMUEL GOLDWYN
The Great Goldwyn by Alva Johnson

My father, who is one hundred years old, tells me every time we set a date to do something together, "I have an excellent memory. As long as I write it down." And he writes down every appointment and remembers it.

This very simple practice of "put it in writing" can go a long way in helping you to maintain a healthy relationship.

When I was first married, my wife, Jo Anne, and I would often make dates with friends for dinner. We would then tell each other over the phone during work or in the evening. This was in those impossibly distant days before email and electronics, and since I had many business meetings as well as social engagements I always carried my paper calendar with me and marked down each activity. Except, of course, when I forgot. When an engagement with friends did not find its way onto Jo Anne's calendar, or mine, we spent hours arguing over whose fault it was. Each of us insisted that the other had forgotten.

Finally, I asked my assistant at the time to type out a copy of each social engagement I made in duplicate. I kept one copy for myself and delivered the other to Jo Anne. The arguments stopped.

My advice to you is simple. If you want to avoid the aggravation of forgetting an appointment or a commitment, put it in writing.

The good news is that putting everything in writing today is much easier than it was years ago. We can text, send an email, or use social media to write anything down and save it, presumably forever.

As an attorney, I remember a time when an agreement only needed to be two or three pages long. That same agreement today might require thirty or forty pages, because today there are more contingencies to be covered. Similarly, relationships are now more complicated than they were even ten years ago. Life moves more quickly, and we all have a lot more to keep track of, so it's more important than ever to put words in writing, especially if they are significant to a relationship.

My father has always told me that if I am willing to promise something I should be willing to write it down and sign my name to it. I think this is good advice, which I follow myself and expect those I deal with in business to respect as well. And this suggestion applies to more than just business. It also applies to your personal life.

A woman I know of is a celebrity who insists that every man she dates sign a confidentiality agreement in which he promises to never reveal anything personal that he may learn about her during their relationship. She asks that he sign this agreement even before their first date. One typical response is, "Are you serious?" She is.

That might be an extreme circumstance, but often it is a very good idea to put an agreement in writing when entering into a long-term relationship. You may avoid unhappy surprises. One of the more prickly examples is the "PreNup" (prenuptual agreement). This is a legal contract, signed before marriage, in which both parties agree on how to divide their property if they should separate or seek a divorce.

I, for one, am a proponent of having a PreNup, even though they can be controversial—especially if there is a substantial difference between the two parties in terms of wealth.

"If you loved me you wouldn't ask me to sign this," is often the position of the partner without property.

"If you loved me for myself you would be happy to sign it," is the predictable response.

My friend Rose, who has considerable wealth, married Ben ten years ago. Ben balked at signing a PreNup, which sent Rose into tears because she thought their wedding plans would have to be cancelled. Ben finally signed. Their marriage is quite happy, so the PreNup remains in the safe deposit box.

My view may be a minority opinion, but I would rather control the conditions of my marriage than leave it up to the state. Let me explain. The day you marry you are, by default, signing a property settlement agreement. That agreement is written into the laws and court decisions of the state in which you marry or live. It's essentially a state-sponsored PreNup, and few of us have any idea about all of its legal provisions. Wouldn't you rather create your own agreement, rather than use the default agreement provided by the state?

I also think it's to your advantage to create a PreNup because at any time, without your knowledge or consent, the laws of the state could change. The legislature might pass new legislation, as California did in 1971, completely changing the rules on marriage. The courts could decide that the existing laws no longer apply, or they could interpret those laws differently and create a new precedent. Thirty years later you might find yourself facing an entirely different set of rules than those in place when you married. During your marriage you might also move to another state or another country where the laws are different.

Reasonable people may differ on this, and the cost of drawing up an agreement may be an obstacle. But at the very least it is important to discuss with your partner your mutual thoughts about what would happen in a breakup. It might seem unthinkable at the time, but we know it is also possible.

Essentially, when you put it in writing you will both will be clear about what will happen if that occurs, and have a better chance of avoiding problems in the future. If you make these important decisions in advance while you are calm and cool-headed it will free you up to focus on what matters most—making your relationship work. You will be able to enjoy being together without the worry and uncertainty of what might happen should you ever part.

I'D RATHER BE ALONE
AND TOGETHER, THAN BE
TOGETHER YET ALONE

You come into this world alone and you go out of this world alone yet it seems to me you are more alone while living than even going and coming.

—EMILY CARR
Hundreds and Thousands: The Journals of Emily Carr

Conversation enriches the understanding, but solitude is the school of genius.

—EDWARD GIBBON
The Decline and Fall of the Roman Empire

From time to time it is fitting for each of us to ask ourselves if our present self-image or life situation still fits. Even though this book is about how to find and share love, and how to succeed in relationships, I do not believe that life is automatically better with an intimate partner.

For many years I studied with Dr. Paul Ware, a psychiatrist who worked in Shreveport, Louisiana. He offered excellent advice on many topics. One of the most important lessons I learned from him was that to create a successful "we," each partner must contain the capacity to live well independently. Only when you are confident in your individuality you can allow yourself to enter fully into a profound partnership. Because you have achieved a level of individual strength and contentment, you will not fear being "swallowed up" by your partner.

When I was young, women married at an average age of twenty and men at twenty-two. Dr. Ware, however, made the sensible observation that before settling into a permanent relationship you should hold your own job, earn your own money, and acquire the confidence that you can take care of yourself. If you miss this step, part of your growth as an autonomous adult will be missing, and you can more easily fall into the trap of believing that your partner should be the foundation of every dimension of your life—financial, emotional, and physical. Fortunately, today the average age of marriage in the United States has risen to twenty-nine for men and twenty-seven for women. This means that both partners are far more likely to have experienced self-sufficiency before they settle down with a partner and establish an "us."

Dr. Ware also taught me that if you depend on just one person to meet more than sixty percent of your emotional needs, you might be headed for grief. You have to become a strong "me" in order to become half of a successful "us."

Rita, who was class valedictorian in my high school graduating class, married her sweetheart Ross one day after she graduated. She married so quickly to escape an unhappy home, where she was the oldest child and was expected to cook, clean, and take care of her younger siblings while babysitting four nights a week to earn her own money for clothing and personal expenses. Rita wanted a better life.

Unfortunately, Rita fled into a living nightmare. Ross, like her family, saw in Rita his own personal slave. Why not? She could do it all, so he didn't bother to hold a job himself or to support his wife emotionally. Ross preferred to hang out with his unemployed friends during the day, later demanding beer and snacks as he watched TV at night. Their marriage was in no sense an "us." It was Rita taking care of a selfish grown-up child who was not capable of either appreciating her or supporting her in any way.

Rita was with another and yet alone.

After Ross pushed Rita against their kitchen table during an argument one night, sending her to the hospital, she finally left him. Sometime later Rita told me, "I'm much better off by myself. It was a hard lesson I had to learn. I'm not even dating now because I need to take care of myself. I find it difficult to trust. I don't know if I'll ever be ready for another relationship."

As William Congreve wrote, "Married in haste, we may repent at leisure."

Some people are just better off "alone" than in a relationship, or at least in a specific relationship. Also, spending time together is not the same as living together full-time. Darlene met Bill on the train from Paris to Berlin when she was twenty-five. They traveled together in Europe for a week, and their encounter was so extraordinary that back in the United States they decided to live together. Just four days later Darlene kicked him out. Spending time with each other while on vacation worked well. Living together was a disaster.

My friend Gloria just turned seventy-seven. Three years ago she decided to sell her home where she had lived by herself for twenty years after a marriage of almost thirty years. Her ex-husband was blind, which is one reason it took her so long to leave him. During her final married years Gloria earned a PhD in nursing in order to support herself, but while they were still together she felt more and more alone.

Today Gloria lives in her own apartment in a Birmingham, Alabama, retirement community where she has met many new friends. "I hardly have time to myself," she says. "Everyone wants to have dinner with me or go to concerts and lectures with me. I'm quite popular, and though I'm living alone, I'm having the best time of my life."

Get yourself together, before you get together with someone else. Being alone is not always easy. But being together with another, and yet still alone, can be far worse.

WEAVE, DON'T LEAVE

To leave is to die a little.
—EDMOND HARAUCOURT
"Rondel de l' Adieu," *Choix de Poésies*

Love me tender, love me sweet,
Never let me go.
—ELVIS PRESLEY
"Love Me Tender"

There is a time in every intimate relationship when the fabric begins to loosen—a time when you and your partner may find yourselves close to shredding the shared tapestry of your life together. Challenges such as money, job, or children may feel overwhelming. At such a time you may want to get out. Or one of you may have met a more exciting potential partner. In these difficult times, I suggest that you stay a while and try with your partner to mend the material of your lives together. I'm saying Weave, Don't Leave.

In my first marriage I failed to weave. This is not something I am proud of and I hope, by sharing this story, to help you learn from my mistake.

Several years into our marriage, I met another woman in the graduate school program I was attending. Her name was Martha, and I fell in love with her. Who wouldn't have? She was smart, sexy, and wrote the most amazing love letters I have ever read.

Again, this is not something I am proud of, but I am here to share my experiences with you, both favorable and flawed, so that you might learn from both.

Eventually I decided to leave my wife and three young children to live with Martha. We spent one night together.

The very next morning Martha called me at my office.

"We've got to talk."

"Okay. Lunch today?"

"Yes. Noon."

"Noon. The usual place." I had no idea what was on her mind.

At lunch she handed me my packed suitcase and said, "I can't do this."

"You can't do what?"

"I can't live with you."

And so began the most traumatic twenty-four hours of my life. We talked for hours. Finally, Martha convinced me that she had made a mistake and was not able to live with me, even though we had planned it that way. She said she just couldn't commit to anyone. I had no wish to impose on Martha, or anyone, who didn't want me. I felt I had no other choice, and left the restaurant in tears.

After our lunch I was supposed to be in class, so I drove to the campus, parked my car, and then wandered around, dazed, from place to place. After an hour or two I noticed a car tracking me. It was my wife's Pontiac. She was taking graduate classes too. And she was watching me.

She pulled up beside me and rolled down her window to talk. I was embarrassed, distraught, and angry. I felt stupid and abandoned. We talked briefly and I got into her car. My wife drove us home. That was one of the most compassionate acts I have experienced in my life.

The next morning I awoke next to my wife in bed, but I didn't move. I felt trapped in my own body and saw no reason to do anything.

"Alan. Get up. Is something wrong?"

I struggled to answer, but I couldn't muster any words. My wife continued to plead. Finally, when I still failed to respond, she called Martha. This time my wife had given me the greatest kindness that I have ever received.

Martha arrived an hour later. I still hadn't moved when she appeared next to me in my bedroom at home.

"Alan. It's okay," she said. She touched my arm and looked at me with concern. I realized what I must have known all along: I had to move past my heartbreak and get on with my life. There is a scene in a Kurt Vonnegut novel where a man walking along a street in New York City stops for no apparent reason. He sees no reason to continue, so he just stands on the sidewalk, frozen. Forty-five minutes later a cop taps him with a baton. "Hey buddy. Move along." Now he sees no reason not to, and resumes the flow of his life. That was exactly how I felt.

From this experience I have derived two rules.

First, I will never again leave one partner for another. The new, the unknown, have all the promise in the world. But the unknown carries peril with its promise. Even more important, I have established a pattern of staying, rather than running away.

Second, I will work on the relationship I have. After leaving two wives and one live-in girlfriend, I realized that something wasn't working in my own process. The problem was not just "them." It was also me. And this is why, for almost thirty-five years, I have committed to working on my present marriage. Just as I said, I will never again leave one partner for another. I will do everything I can to make the relationship I have work.

To this day I remember Martha, and from time to time I think of her. But, as she wrote to me more than forty years ago, "Dreams are extremely fragile outside the womb of the mind."

Weave, Don't Leave.

SETTLE, SETTLE, SETTLE

Love doesn't just sit there, like a stone, it has to be made,
like bread; re-made all the time, made new.
— URSULA LE GUIN
The Lathe of Heaven

Marriages are made in Heaven and consummated on Earth.
— JOHN LYLY
Mother Bombie act IV (1590)

The title of this chapter was inspired by a joke about a tourist lost in Times Square. He sees a man rushing by who is carrying a violin case and asks, "Can you tell me how to get to Carnegie Hall?"

The man with the violin case sighs, and says, "Practice, practice, practice."

That is good advice for anything you want to improve in, whether it's playing the violin, cooking a turkey for Thanksgiving, or enjoying a great relationship.

For some reason many of us assume that we will succeed in our relationships without actually working at them. Maybe this is because we've done it before. All of us have had successful relationships with friends, teachers, coworkers, and fellow riders on the bus. Those experiences create an assumption of mastery. But the most important relationships—the ones in which we share our lives, our families, our

141

homes, and our beds—are much more challenging. And to succeed they require Practice, Practice, Practice.

I say this because I have been married to three very different women and lived with another. I have traveled with many people, family and otherwise. I am seventy-five years old, and I still work at improving my relationships every day. I have earned a master's degree in counseling, and still I am not a master. I haven't gotten it entirely right yet, which is why I'm still practicing. So don't be embarrassed to say, if only to yourself, "Yes, I'm working at it, but I haven't quite got this relationship stuff one hundred percent perfect. I still have an exciting way to go."

One of the best ways to "practice, practice, practice" in your relationship is to learn how to "Settle, Settle, Settle."

If you think I am going to ask you to settle for less than a perfect relationship or life, I am. But before you close your mind on the subject, let me make my case.

The first of the three Settles is that you have to settle into your relationship, blending your interests and your differences. This takes time, whether a week, a month, or, more likely, years. There is so much to negotiate. Who gets the top drawer? Will you share the same bedroom, or not? Who gets the right side of the bed? (That would be me.) What brand of toothpaste do you buy? Are you going to be on time as a couple, or late? Will you go to bed at 9:00 p.m. or 2:00 a.m.? Is it important for both of you to go to bed together? How do you, as a couple, handle money? Do you prefer joint bank accounts or separate finances? If sex is part of your relationship, what do you like? How much and how often?

As I mentioned in a previous chapter, Dr. Paul Ware of Shreveport, Louisiana, is a psychiatrist I studied with years ago. He told me the story of a shrimp boat captain who insisted on making love with his wife three times a day. Yes, he even returned home from the sea for lunch, and not for a home-cooked meal. By the time they were in their fifties, his wife complained.

"Dr. Ware," she said, "three times a day is too much."

With Paul as a mediator, the couple compromised. The husband agreed that he would remain on his boat for lunch.

You have to get used to each other. This the first Settle. Settle in.

The next Settle is this: Settle for less than your idea of perfection, unless, of course, you are perfect and want perfect company (hint: you won't find any).

Even if your partner seems to be your perfect soul mate, he or she will still take actions you won't like from time to time, such as arriving home three hours late without calling or texting, or failing to write down in the checkbook all checks and deposits. You will have differences to resolve, and you will not change everything about your partner's behavior. If you think you can, please write and explain to me why you are still arguing about the same topic for two, or six, or twenty-five years. Why are you now having the same arguments you had with a previous partner? To maintain a successful relationship it is critical for both partners to learn how to navigate through the differences that will inevitably arise between you on an ongoing basis.

If you or your partner has a core issue (something on which you will absolutely not compromise), such as no smoking, then there shouldn't be a fight. There is just an ultimatum. But short of that, you are going to have to settle for less than everything you want. Does your boss, or did your parent, give you everything you wanted? My father tells me that his parents refused to give him the moon, even though he threw repeated tantrums to persuade them. When you disagree on a core issue that neither party will compromise on, you will need to decide if you both can live with that gulf in your values.

This brings us to the final Settle, which you will only encounter if the core values between you cannot be resolved and you have decided to live apart.

If you separate from each other, Settle. Settle your financial and/or other issues quickly, and settle them courteously. If you or your (former) partner want to fight for a year or for a lifetime, you will be stuck in each other's lives for what will seem like eternity, and you will support the legal profession until you run out of money.

Years ago my friend Donna showed me an offer from Todd, her soon to be ex-husband.

"This is the offer," she said. "And here is the letter from my attorney telling me that Todd's offer is much too low and he won't represent me anymore if I take it."

I studied the agreement. I happened to know Todd and his finances well.

"His offer looks reasonable to me," I said. "And, if you accept it, of course your attorney won't represent you anymore. He won't need to. No more fighting. He'll have to bill other clients for his time."

Donna accepted Todd's proposal. Five years later, when her agreed-upon spousal support ended, Todd volunteered to continue helping Donna financially. And, as far as I know, they remain good friends to this day.

Filene, on the other hand, remains locked in legal limbo with her ex-husband Doug ten years after their divorce. They are still arguing about child support, spousal support, and child custody. Perhaps fortunately, their dog died. Unfortunately, just as in the tango, it takes two to Settle.

To be successful at most activities you need to practice, practice, practice. This is true if you are trying to get to Carnegie Hall and it is true if you are trying to build and maintain a healthy relationship with the love of your life. But in the latter, it is equally important to remember that you will need to learn to settle: into the relationship, into each other's differences, and finally, when all else fails, into each other's past.

YOURS, OURS, AND MINE

Sharing a bed and a future was child's play compared to sharing my copy of The Complete Poems of W.B. Yeats.

—ANNE FADIMAN
"Marrying Libraries," *Ex Libris Confessions of a Common Reader*

I share no man's opinions. I have my own.

—IVAN SERGEYEVICH TURGENEV
Fathers and Sons

Food can be a very important part of your relationship. You share meals, you share a grocery bill, you share restaurant visits, and you share a refrigerator. So much of the time spent together and many of the decisions in your relationship will revolve around this most basic human need.

I recently visited my dentist's office for my semiannual teeth cleaning and was greeted by a new dental hygienist.

"I'm Sally," she said, "and I will be taking care of you today."

Oh, joy. I offered her my standard reply: "I'll make you the same deal I made with Eleanor who was here for years. You don't hurt me, I don't bite you."

Sally stared at me.

I continued. "Eleanor must have retired because she had only three fingers left on her working hand."

Sally smiled.

"I think we'll get along just fine," she said.

I wondered about that. Her "fine" or mine? Have you ever noticed that unlike your hairdresser or your barber, conversations with your dental hygienist seem to go only one way? He or she talks, you grunt. It's never an equal sharing of either information or ideas.

I opened wide. Sally poked around with her instruments of torture. Surprisingly, she didn't hurt me a bit. (Past tense of "bite." It's a bad pun.)

Then she started to work in earnest, and while she toiled away on my teeth she chattered incessantly. Within ten minutes she revealed her entire life history ending with this:

"I lived by myself for twenty years. Then a year and a half ago I married Roland. He is great, but he has two teenage children who live with their mother and visit our house on Wednesday evenings and weekends."

I grunted understanding.

"The problem is that they always eat my food. The three of them are always on a strict diet, so they like my food, which I buy for myself, more than what they usually eat. It tastes better than theirs. One day I was salivating all afternoon thinking about my favorite dinner. I could taste it. I could smell it. I drove home, opened the refrigerator, and it wasn't there. Roland or one of his children had eaten it."

I grunted sympathy.

"That didn't work for me. I was not happy. I talked to Roland about it, and I told him that no one touches my food."

Sally gave me a small plastic cup of water.

"Spit," she said.

I did, and was able to get in a few words. "That's a tough problem. It's tricky to live with someone else after living by yourself for years. Especially when there are kids. That's not easy. Have you worked it out?"

"Yes. I made it very clear to Roland that he and his sons had to stop eating my food. Or else . . . Now they don't touch my food without my permission."

Though I do give ultimatums at home myself from time to time, it is never without a concern for the consequences. Daveen is somewhat resistant to being told what to do. Or not to do. Ultimatums in my house have been known to backfire. Badly. On me.

Like all couples, Daveen and I have our differences. Fortunately food isn't one of them. And we have learned how to share. We separate what is hers from what is mine, and we share what is ours in a way that allows us both to feel good. For example, we each have an automatic veto over art displayed on the walls of our home. While we share a great deal, we each have our own electronics, and there are some things we don't particularly want the other to share. Like a cold. Or a painting that one of us dislikes!

One habit I learned from my mother is that if you want to fill both the fridge and the pantry with food that you like, go to the grocery store and buy it yourself. I always joined my mother when she went grocery shopping. I was a hungry kid, and I was always figuring out how to get what I wanted. I wanted Mom to buy the food I liked, which is why I went with her. And I taught myself how to cook. Today I have a separate shelf in our refrigerator and a separate section of our freezer. When I want to heat my frozen split pea soup for dinner I, like Sally, don't want to discover that my soup has disappeared.

Daveen and I do not share every waking moment, every fleeting thought, or every morsel of food. The extent of privacy, or sharing, is different in every relationship, and you and your partner can and should talk about and decide these issues for yourselves.

In my family of origin we typically take food from each other's plates, without asking. For me your half-eaten steak or your last bite of cake is fair game. My brother once dated a woman who was appalled at the idea of community food. And today Daveen abhors "double dipping" from the guacamole.

I can't say that my brother's date or Daveen are wrong. In fact, they are right. Just as each nation and each group has its own culture, each family has its own rules. We determine our preferences when we are young, and those patterns do persist. (See "Patterns Persist" in People Tools.)

Sally and Roland are on the right track. They compromised. (That means Roland gave in, which is what "compromise" often means.) Attach a note to the Tupperware dish of leftover tuna salad if you want to keep it for yourself. And if you don't want someone else to use your special shampoo, designate it as "off limits."

Many of the possessions and much of the time of our lives is "ours." But some thoughts, some food, and the right side of the bed are mine. No "ifs," "ands," or "bits" (the same pun coming to bit you in the butt again) about it.

THE GET OUT-OF-JAIL-PRACTICALLY-FREE CARD

Forgiveness to the injured does belong;
But they ne'er pardon who have done the wrong.

—JOHN DRYDEN
The Conquest of Granada (1670)

Pray you now, forget and forgive.

—SHAKESPEARE
King Lear

Over the course of your relationship, you and your partner will occasionally transgress. I might leave my socks on the floor of the bathroom. Daveen might, once in a great while, pick me up late at my office. Neither of us is perfect. In the case of small transgressions, I suggest that a little forgiveness will go a long way.

I propose that on the first day of each calendar month you give each other a three-by-five index card that says, "Any time during this month you may give me this card and Get out of Jail Practically Free."

Before you give it to your partner, sign and date the card.

There are just two rules.

First, when you choose to use the card for something forgivable, your partner must immediately let go of being upset about whatever it is you did or didn't do. The disagreement is over.

Second, this card does not cover all transgressions. It's a *practically free* card. It is up to your partner to decide whether or not the offense is forgivable enough for you to use the card as your sincere apology, and let the issue go.

At this point you might be thinking, "Well, what if my partner is unreasonable and always refuses to accept the card, or won't give me one in the first place?"

This is meant to be a good faith exercise in forgiveness in an otherwise healthy relationship. If you don't trust your partner to be reasonable, or if your partner does not trust you to be reasonable, then one or both of you should think about whether you have the partnership that you really want and deserve.

But since you have only one "practically free" card a month, you might want be more careful with each other. If you are like me, you will hoard your card for most of the month, just in case something more serious comes along. And if neither of you feels the need to use your card, voilà! You must have shared a great month.

Every fulfilling relationship requires mutual trust. The "Get-Out-of-Jail-Practically-Free" card is a concrete way to demonstrate and build that trust. If you don't need it, the trust is already there.

If you want to go for the stars, on the first day of each year you might give your partner a signed and dated card that says, "Happy New Year. I love you and commit to stay with you this year and, I hope, forever." (You might want to leave out the "I hope" part.) Give this card freely, and you will never need one in return.

ASK AND BE THANKFUL

Reflect on your present blessings—of which every man has many—
Not on your past misfortunes, of which all men have some.
—CHARLES DICKENS
A Christmas Dinner

Gratitude, n. A sentiment lying midway between
a benefit received and benefit expected.
—AMBROSE BIERCE
The Wasp (San Francisco), May 28, 1885

Every long-term relationship, even one that begins with romantic lights and soft music, may at some point start to seem less than ideal. You may even find that your partner has one or two habits that bother you (heaven forbid!).

When this happens, you might gather your courage to speak up about whatever it is you would like your partner to do differently. For example, imagine the following conversation: "Darling, I really would appreciate your putting the mail where I can see it, rather than in your purse or in your car."

Let's assume the best, and that you don't even have to mention past transgressions. There is no need to say: "What do I have to do? Move to a new address and pick up my mail myself?"

Let's also assume that your partner (who in this scenario is every bit as wonderful as he or she could possibly be) instantly sees both the wisdom of your words and the wrongness of his or her actions.

151

"Yes, dear. I will be rigorous in picking up the mail every single day and leaving anything addressed to you right under the fruit bowl where you can see it as soon as you come in every evening. No more delaying the delivery of your junk mail by leaving it in my car or throwing it out entirely."

What should you say in reply?

"Thank you."

Then, in your fantasy world, the partner might continue:

"Yes, dear. I am so, so, so very sorry. I only want to serve you, and my fervent wish is that you had told me this months ago so that I could have amended my ways earlier and continued to please you in every facet of our relationship all of the time."

As you already know, this scene is pure fantasy. It has never happened to me, nor to anyone I know. But what happens next may be a reality. Your reality.

The next day, and the next week, your partner leaves your mail precisely as you have requested. Now is it time for . . .

"Well, it's about time! I've been asking you to do this for an entire year. Ever since you lost the credit card bill which cost us a penalty of seventy five dollars."

Whoops! This is not good form. Never allow yourself to let the words "it's about time," fly out of your mouth, even if you're thinking them. You can never take words back, and they may trigger your partner to "lose" your mail for the next few years. Instead, express sincere appreciation.

So when you ask, with love and consideration, and you are rewarded with the performance or words which you request, there is only one response that will cause the lights to dim again and the soft music to filter over you and your love. I hope you know exactly which two words I am talking about. They are:

"Thank you."

It's that simple. Ask, receive, and be thankful. In this way, you can build your own fantastic reality: a life of love and shared memories.

WAITING FOR GODOT

It is circumstance and proper timing that give an action its character and make it either good or bad.

—"LIFE OF AGESILAUS"
Plutarch's Lives

Some are born mad. Some remain so.

—SAMUEL BECKETT
Waiting for Godot

Many years ago, when my parents arrived at my house for a visit, they were always in the midst of the very same argument.

"Why can't you be on time?!?!?!" my father would fume.

"I couldn't find my purse," my mother would say.

But the purse excuse didn't matter. Nor did losing track of time or looking for her glasses. If it wasn't one reason for being late, it was another. When it came to time, my mother clearly marched to the beat of her own drummer. Did I mention that when I was young she was always between ten minutes and an hour late when she picked me up from school?

My father was the opposite. He was a professional musician and played the French horn in many orchestras, including the Los Angeles Philharmonic. To keep his job, Dad had to be on time. My father is now one hundred years old, and the other day he told me that he felt he was "slowing down" a little. If she were still alive (and so inclined), maybe Mom would now keep up with him.

Time, it turns out, is a common source of stress in a relationship. And it's rare that both partners share exactly the same relationship to it.

When Daveen and I moved in together, it became apparent that I was living with a woman who, like my mother, also marched to the beat of her own drummer. Daveen was late sometimes. It really doesn't matter why. It was just her nature at that time.

The first time my parents came to our house for dinner they arrived at 5:00 p.m. on a Sunday afternoon. After twenty minutes my father discreetly asked, "Where's Daveen?"

"Dad, she's at the market shopping for something to cook for dinner." My mom, dad, and I chatted. It felt like we were characters in Samuel Beckett's play *Waiting for Godot*. Of course, unlike the play, our Godot ultimately did put in an appearance, and we did enjoy dinner together.

As you might have already guessed, unlike Daveen, I tend to march to the same drumbeat as my father. I like to be on time or early. In the early days, months, and years of our relationship, Daveen used to pick me up at the office whenever we were going somewhere after work. We both prefer to drive together, so I would leave my car at home. But when Daveen was late I was infuriated. In fact, I sounded just like my dad shouting at my mom. (I must admit that these days the shoe is on . . . Daveen now often waits for me at the back door of my office building because, well, I have a lot to do which is my way of saying I too lose track of time.)

Fortunately, Daveen and I did not remain stuck in this continuous circle. We solved the problem.

"Daveen," I said, "my mother is always late, and my parents always fight about it. We're not going to do that. When we are leaving from my office, I'm going to have my own car there, and if you don't pick me up on time, we can then meet at the event. When we are supposed to leave from home at 7:00 p.m. I'll be happy to wait for ten minutes.

After that, I'll drive myself. You are welcome to drive yourself to the event, and I will greet you with pleasure. There will be no quarrel. If you decide to stay home, there will be no dispute when I get back. I've seen this fight play out on an endless loop between my parents, and we're not going to box with each other for eternity over our timing."

Daveen wholeheartedly agreed.

I followed up on our agreement only once. Daveen and I had tickets for a play downtown. My daughter Jill and I were ready to leave at 7:00 p.m. I had given Daveen her own ticket before she left in the morning.

At ten minutes past seven Jill and I were seated in my car, just as Daveen whizzed into our double car garage.

"Hi, doll! We're leaving for the play."

"I'll be with you in just three minutes. I have to change. I'll be right there."

"Jill and I are leaving now."

"Then I won't be coming!"

"Either way. I'd be happy to see the play with you, or happy to see you when we get back."

"I'm not going!"

(Caveat: Daveen absolutely, positively tells me she never said this, and never would say this without following through on it. Scientific research clearly indicates that even if you are categorically certain of your memory, you are not necessarily correct. None of us is. So it is certainly possible that Daveen did not say what I remember her saying.

But I'm the writer, and it's a better story my way. I also prefer to stay married. My ninth grade journalism teacher said that you should only believe half of what you read in a newspaper. Of course, he never said which half. So Daveen might well be correct. If I'm wrong, I apologize.)

I waved, and drove off with Jill.

Jill said, "Dad, she seemed really upset. Maybe we should wait for her."

"Jill, there is not going to be a fight about this. I think she'll be there."

"I don't think so, Dad."

Three minutes before the opening curtain Daveen arrived, stunning, in my favorite red dress, and we held hands throughout the performance.

We found an effective alternative to continuing disputes about timing. I drive my own car to the office. Daveen, in turn, is now normally on time. Also, she can talk happily away on her cell phone during those long minutes that it takes me to rush through the office gauntlet. We are both happier as a result, and if either of us is late we still enjoy our evening.

Sometimes you wait for Godot. Sometimes Godot waits for you. In either case life goes on, but no one has to get bent out of shape over out-of-sync timing.

BELT BUCKLE, REVISITED

A man is the origin of his action.

—ARISTOTLE
Nicomachean Ethics Book I

All of our thoughts, words, and promises may deceive us, but our actions are the true statement of our identity.

—ALAN C. FOX
People Tools, Tool 6: "The Belt Buckle"

Most of what I've learned about love and relationships has been through trial and error. After leaving my second wife I realized that something wasn't working in my own process. I knew I needed to figure out what it was before I entered into yet another relationship that would ultimately fail. I spent a great deal of time thinking about this. What was wrong in my method? How could I change my process of selection and take responsibility for my part in those prior relationships? What was my pattern, and how could I prevent myself from repeating it?

Fortunately, I figured out a solution before I met Daveen by using a tool called "The Belt Buckle," which I wrote about in my first book, *People Tools*. "The Belt Buckle" is one of the most important tools in that entire book, and the first chapter I ever wrote. As quoted above, "our actions are the true statement of our identity." So what I had to do was to pay attention to my own actions and, sure enough, a pattern was revealed.

My first wife was the one who asked *me* to the high school "Sadie Hawkins" dance.

My serious live-in girlfriend was the one who initiated our relationship when she invited me to dinner at her apartment.

My second wife invited me to attend a concert with her immediately after our first date.

Clearly, my pattern (or belt buckle) was to leap into a serious relationship with the first woman I was attracted to and who appeared to like me back. I was almost forty before I realized that I had been so insecure I unconsciously believed no woman would ever love me. And so if any woman expressed interest by asking me out, I grabbed her because I was afraid there would never be another. I ignored any and all indications that a serious long-term relationship might not work out.

This was the persistent pattern for my first three significant relationships. Because I was afraid to risk being rejected, I repeatedly made choices that ultimately weren't right for me in the long term.

But thanks to much reflection, I was able to break the pattern with Daveen, who I have now been married to for almost thirty-five years. When we first met I wasn't certain she would ever feel the same way about me as I felt about her. But rather than back away, I took a risk. As we walked to our first lunch together (which I had invited her to), Daveen said that she had very good reasons not to date me. Earlier in my life I would have feared her potential rejection and run away. But this time I persevered, and as a result we began a relationship that has become a long, happy marriage.

If you think you want a long-term relationship but find yourself moving from one partner to another, I suggest you take a look at your own belt buckle. After all, you are the only one who makes your choices. Perhaps you really prefer short-term connections. Or possibly you are basing decisions upon your fear, rather than your affection.

Take a little time to consider your actions before you launch into your next commitment. Observe your belt buckle. If you like where it has led you in the past, then by all means follow it. If not, you might change your approach. This is the only way I know of to break out of a persistent pattern that has failed to give you the result you believe you wanted.

Clearly, I haven't always learned my lesson the first time. This is true for many of us. But to me the objective for a rewarding life is not necessarily to succeed at once. It is to succeed at last.

Belt Buckle, Revisited. It's that important.

YOU ARE MY VALENTINE

How do I love thee? Let me count the ways?
—ELIZABETH BARRETT BROWNING
Sonnets from the Portuguese

Why is it that the most unoriginal thing we can say to one another is still the thing we long to hear? 'I love you' is always a quotation.
—JEANETTE WINTERSON
Written on the Body

If you're a fan of St. Valentine's Day, as I am, then you might wonder whom to thank for this most romantic of days. Through the miracle of Google and Wikipedia I discovered that you should send a card to Geoffrey Chaucer because I found the following:

The "first recorded association of Valentine's Day with romantic love is in *Parlement of Foules* (1382) by Geoffrey Chaucer."

In those days, when spelling was a free-for-all, here is what Chaucer wrote:

For this was on seynt Volantynys day
Whan euery bryd comyth there to chese his make.

("For this was on St. Valentine's Day,
when every bird cometh there to choose his mate.")

Enough history. Fast forward to the present time when, perhaps, this holiday has surrendered part of its original luster to commercial interests. The sentiments expressed in most of today's Valentine's Day cards tend to be hesitant. "Will you be my Valentine?" "Please be my Valentine." "I miss you, Valentine."

I suggest that you take a more direct and confident approach and simply say:

YOU ARE MY VALENTINE!

Every woman wants to hear that. So does every man. No guessing, no games, just a candid and definitive declaration.

When I was in law school, after a full year in a contracts class, the professor revealed that the real secret to crafting a binding contract was to state at the end of the written document: "And I mean it, gosh darn it." (I paraphrase.)

So you might add to the simple statement above three inspiring words, such as "I love you." A dozen red roses, or candy, would be another nice touch, for which retailers will love you.

You could even be a contrarian and recognize that a Valentine's Day card is much more unusual, and even more appreciated, on some other day of the year. Why wait for a specific holiday to recognize those nearest your heart? Why not tell them every single day of the year? It is never too early or too late to let your sweetheart, children, or close friends know how much you cherish them. Few of us ever tire of being told that we are loved, or that we are special. So make every day a holiday. You can tell your partner every single morning and every single night: "You Are My Valentine, and I love you." And then you can celebrate each day as if it were a special occasion, which it is.

My wife likes to start celebrating a few days or months early, so I'm busy now for the rest of the evening. I'll see you at Easter, bunny.

THE EMPTY THEATER

This whole creation is essentially subjective, and the dream is the theater where the dreamer is at once scene, actor, prompter, stage manager, author, audience, and critic.

—CARL GUSTAV JUNG
Psychological Reflections: A Jung Anthology

*All the world's a stage.
And all the men and women merely players.*

—WILLIAM SHAKESPEARE
As You Like It

If you've spent much time with young children, you have likely seen an infant or toddler crying brokenheartedly, but pausing to look around and see if anyone is noticing. In short, the child is acting simply to gain sympathy.

Each of us is sometimes that child, playing the scene not out of some internal need, but merely to influence the audience. When I'm angry, I have been known to walk around the house, peeking to see if Daveen is noticing. Sometimes I've thought of an excuse to walk into the room where she is so that she will see my scowl and know I am upset. With her. I've noticed that my glare tends to disappear when she is out running errands and there's no audience for my anger.

This is good news. It means that I am in charge of the face I choose to show the world, and current research reveals that a smile actually increases the flow of endorphins in the brain, which elevates your mood. So the face I choose to show to the world is now a pleasant one, regardless of how I felt before smiling, because I am always ready for a cheerful contact.

Why do I do this? Because I'm a pragmatist. I want a positive result. I want whoever sees me to feel welcome and free to share with me whatever they have in mind. I will never win the Academy Award as "Best Actor," or even "Best Supporting Actor," but I do win the reward of happiness every single day.

I am not talking about putting on an "act." I am talking about being authentic. In the theater of my life I try to share my joy, my fear, and my grief accurately and completely with others who are my audience. That's what life is about—fully participating, up close and personal.

Many years ago when I was in the middle of my first divorce, I agreed to drive twenty miles to a meet a group of doctors who were potential investors. Even though I was an emotional wreck, I was just starting out in commercial real estate and needed all the investors I could find, so I would speak to anyone, anywhere.

I was able to put my personal feelings aside, and the evening went well. I answered all of the doctors' questions, and four or five of them gave me their contact information so that I could notify them about future investments. As I left the building I was elated.

While driving back to my one-room apartment, my delight darkened to despair. There was no one at home with whom I could share my triumph, no one I could brag to or celebrate with. There was no one who would be excited about the prospect of our having a better life together. I wanted to continue being the star of the show, but I was returning to an empty theater.

But this raises the question: Does it matter if the theater is empty or full? Should that change how I act or how I experience my life?

Years ago I read a remarkable story about a soprano at an opera house in Nevada. Not only did she perform there every evening, six or seven nights a week for many years, almost until her death. She also cleaned the small auditorium, sold the tickets, and with no help from anyone put on her costumes and applied her stage makeup. Then she would take the stage and sing, even if not a single person was in the audience, which was often the case. I call that living a full, rich, and dedicated life. She was doing what she loved.

The world is a theater (even though it sometimes may be the theater of the absurd). Sometimes many of the seats are occupied, whether in the front row or in the balcony. From time to time, the house is full. Occasionally it is empty.

The People Tool of "The Empty Theater" means that you always show up and present your authentic self, regardless of who is in the audience. You are not some hack actor who imitates life. The true test of your performance is not when every seat is taken, but when you are alone, living your life fully and sincerely, even though the theater may be, temporarily, unfilled.

ABANDON SHIP

A relationship, I think, is, is like a shark, you know, it has to con-stantly move forward or it dies, and I think what we got on our hands is a dead shark.

ALVY SINGER, PLAYED BY WOODY ALLEN IN THE FILM, IS SPEAKING
—Annie Hall

It hurts to let go. Sometimes it seems the harder you try to hold on to something or someone the more it wants to get away.

—HENRY ROLLINS
The Portable Henry Rollins

No matter how compatible you and your partner may be, there will always be subjects on which you disagree. You may both love skiing, cooking, and going to movies together. You may want the same number of children, or no children at all. You may share similar values around family, money, and religion.

But in spite of your similarities, you will eventually find a dis-agreement. Many couples are able to successfully navigate through their differences and find a common ground on which to build a strong relationship. But those differences may become seemingly irreconcilable, and you could find yourself facing a tough question: Is it time to abandon ship?

Gwen is one of my closest friends. She has treated me to lunch for many years. She and her ex-husband Stan raised five children dur-ing their long marriage.

During their first years together, those wild Southern California days of the late sixties and early seventies, Gwen and Stan lived the good life, overindulging in everything—wild parties, drugs, and alcohol. But the activities that appealed to them in their twenties became less compelling when Gwen and Stan matured into their forties, with one exception. Stan liked to drink and refused to give up his nightly bottle of wine, accompanied by hard liquor. One afternoon Gwen telephoned me. She was in tears.

"Alan, I can't take it anymore. The drugs and alcohol were fun, but at this point I've given them up. Stan still drinks, and when he does he's abusive—not physically, but emotionally. I can't live like this any longer, and I'm going to tell Stan that unless he stops drinking I'll leave him." It sounded like unless Stan changed his behavior Gwen was going to change her address.

This was a surprise to me, but not an uncommon situation. Weeks went by, then months. They remained together.

A year later Gwen said, "He stopped drinking for a while, but then he started again. But he doesn't drink as much as he used to."

Some time after that Gwen called me and repeated our first conversation, practically word for word.

"Alan, he's drinking more and more every night. I'm giving him one final chance, but if he doesn't stop drinking completely I'll have to leave."

He didn't, and she did. What followed, predictably, were five years of unpleasant divorce proceedings—sorting out finances, negotiating child custody, and healing emotional wounds.

Though most of us may enter into a relationship with the hope and expectation that it will be forever, you never really know how long any partnership will last. The ultimate question may arise, "Should I leave? Should I abandon ship?"

The very idea of departing is distasteful to most of us. In many situations the partner who wants to leave does not want to take responsibility. He, or she, does not want friends or family to point to them as the reason for a split. Rather than just leaving, they may follow the devious course of being unpleasant for as long as it takes, hoping that eventually their partner will want to escape.

My acquaintance Lynne was, and is, a devoted woman who lives honorably and loves with her whole heart. When she was seventeen she married a twenty-three-year-old Marine named Larry. Larry was physically abusive. Lynne told me on one occasion Larry was actually trying to strangle her, with both of his hands around her neck.

"As I passed out, I thought, 'This is it. This time I'm going to die,'" she said.

But Lynne remained loyal, and stayed with Larry for four years. When she finally left she changed her name and moved half-way across the country so he couldn't find her and kill her. At age thirty Lynne married for the second time, and now has one of the happiest marriages of anyone I know. And her new husband has never struck her.

In this case, or any instance of repeated physical or emotional abuse, it may be appropriate to Abandon Ship sooner rather than later. This may be difficult and require advance planning, but accepting punishment should never be part of being in love.

In my first *People Tools* book, one of the first chapters is entitled "Patterns Persist." I suggested that you adapt the practice of noticing the patterns of performance in other people, and understand that you should expect those patterns to continue. A disorganized person will remain disorganized, a careful driver will remain a careful driver. If you expect your partner to change in any major way, your chance of building a harmonious "us" is, to say the least, limited.

My company used to manage more than four thousand apartment units. One fine July, on the first of the month, an apartment manager stole all of the cash he had collected from tenants. My rule is, "Steal once and you're gone." Two weeks later I spoke with the manager's supervisor.

"I assume that the manager is gone."

"Well, not exactly."

"What do you mean, 'not exactly.' You know our policy."

"Yes, but the manager really needs the job, and his wife had unexpected medical bills. He regarded the money as a loan, and promised me personally that he would pay it back by the end of the month. So I let him stay."

Yes, you know how this story ends. On the first of the following month the manager had not repaid a cent, and stole even more money. This time I fired him myself and reported his theft to the police.

While it is important to work on any major relationship (see "Weave, Don't Leave"), if you find significant problems that you don't feel you can overcome in the early stages, I encourage you to cut your losses quickly and make room in your life for someone better suited to you.

There is a saying that another person is in your life for a reason, a season, or a lifetime. I highly value the "for a lifetime" part. These are the relationships that bring the greatest satisfaction into my life. And that is why I recommend that you try to reconcile your differences if at all possible. But at some point you may need to Abandon Ship, even from the most important relationship of your life. But please be thoughtful about it. We both know that the water out there can be icy. But if the time ever comes, don't be too frightened to leap.

IT'S A MOVIE,
NOT A SNAPSHOT

Love itself is what is left over when being in love has burned away.
—LOUIS DE BERNIERES
Captain Corelli's Mandolin

The course of true love never did run smooth.
—WILLIAM SHAKESPEARE
Troilus and Cressida

Shortly after Daveen and I began living together we piled our six assorted children into a VW Bus and drove to Crater Lake, Oregon. We rented a cabin for two nights with a beautiful view of the lake.

On the first night of our trip I was reading in bed when Daveen slipped under the covers. Instead of feeling my usual flood of warmth towards her, I had a strange and unexpected reaction. I felt no connection to her at all. I felt as if she was a complete stranger. Needless to say, I was dismayed and wondered what to do.

My first thought was to act as if nothing had happened, as if I felt exactly the same way about her as I had the night before and the night before that. At work I was an expert at ignoring problems that scared me, stuffing them into an emotional lockbox with no key. Sometimes a dilemma disappeared over time, and I never had to think about it again. But I also knew that a relationship, especially a relatively new one, is fragile, and that the core of trust that must build over years can be lost in one moment of deceit.

My next idea was to share my feeling with Daveen, even at the risk of alarming her. Did I trust her to hang in there with me until my attachment to her returned? Would it return? I had never felt this distant from any other woman I had been close to. It has been said that "not to decide is to decide," and it was clear to me that my situation was precarious. If I didn't immediately say something I would be choosing to pretend. I had to decide which was the lesser evil, and decide quickly.

In retrospect I believe this may have been a turning point in our relationship. Conceal or reveal. That was the question.

I decided to tell her.

"Daveen, I have something to share with you."

"Sure, honey. What is it?"

I felt like I was back in college, where I was required to take a class in swimming. One condition for passing the class was to dive off the high board. Every time we lined up for the high dive, as soon as I reached the head of the line I would wander toward the back and allow everyone else to go ahead of me. In this way I had never actually practiced a single high dive. Not one.

Then it was time for the final exam. After I swam several laps using different strokes, the instructor pointed to the high diving board.

"I'd rather not."

"Really? You'd rather not? Do you want to pass the class, or take it again?"

"I'd like to pass, sir."

Again, he motioned to the high board.

I was terrified, but realized that to graduate from college I would, at some point, have to do this. Shaking, I climbed the rungs and stepped onto the board. I ran to the end of the board, closed my eyes, and dove into the water. As I fell toward the water I felt exactly how I now felt in bed at Crater Lake. Panicked.

"Daveen, a really strange feeling came over me as you were getting into bed. It may have started this afternoon. For some reason, I just don't feel connected to you. You seem like a stranger, like some anonymous guest who should be sleeping in another room."

"Did I do something wrong?"

"No. Not at all. I don't understand it. I can't think of a single reason I should feel this way. But I do."

"Okay. What do you want me to do?"

Our conversation was going better than I had feared. Daveen wasn't reacting with hostility or defensiveness. She was just listening. "Nothing. You don't need to do anything. I just thought that I should tell you. I don't want to fake my feelings for you. I think and hope that my sense of being cut off from you will fade, but I don't really know."

Daveen was her usual cheerful self. "O.K. Do you mind if we snuggle?"

"I would like that." We did. After a time I fell asleep.

Two or three days later my feeling that Daveen and I were an "us" returned and has remained with me ever since.

There are moments in every relationship—moments of doubt, moments of anger, moments of separation—in which any one of us might wonder if there is still an "us." Those moments are like a photo. The action is frozen in time.

But a relationship is not a snapshot. It is a series of moments, a video. And we don't go out Saturday night to see a photo. We buy our ticket to see a movie, a motion picture with a beginning, a middle, and an end.

When a photograph in any relationship is scary, please remember that it is not your life. It is just one moment in your life. You cannot know how it will, or will not, be resolved. So stick it out.

Be terrified if you will, close your eyes if you must, but assume that in your future there will continue to be an "us" and the movie will have a happy ending. And the more you reveal to your partner at the critical moment in a relationship, the greater your chance of a rewarding resolution. But I'm not sure I would recommend a night at Crater Lake.

KEEP IN ORBIT

Bright star, would I were steadfast as thou art—
—JOHN KEATS
First line of the sonnet "Bright Star"

"For a breeze of morning moves,
And the planet of Love is on high,
Beginning to faint in the light that she loves
On a bed of daffodil sky."
—ALFRED, LORD TENNYSON
"Maud"

I recently attended a concert at the Edinburgh Festival by the BBC Scottish Symphony Orchestra performing Holst's *The Planets*. I started thinking about the planets orbiting around the sun. Then I thought about relationships.

In any intimate relationship, you and your partner orbit around each other like binary stars, bound together by the gravity of your passion. As I reflected on this, I realized that a relationship, like those two stars, must achieve an extraordinary balance between pull and push in order to stay in orbit. On one hand, you have to avoid the pull between you becoming so strong that you slam into each other and become a single bit of cosmic dust with no individuality. On the other hand, you need to maintain enough attraction so you don't fly off to a remote part of the galaxy.

One of the most common ways to fall out of orbit and merge unhappily with each other happens when one partner tries to control the other. For example, when I was first married I was extremely concerned about the behavior of my wife at parties, even though she was quite well-behaved. For some reason, I worried that if she ever said or did something inappropriate that I would be blamed. It was tough enough for me to monitor my own words and actions. Though I followed her like a shadow, it was, of course, impossible for me to control my wife's every action.

I have since come to understand that in a binary relationship my partner and I must allow ourselves to be the separate individuals that we are, without trying to control the other. I would not want Daveen to sit and stare at me in my office all day long, and she doesn't want me watching over her shoulder while she negotiates for an upgrade of our airplane seats. We each need space and trust each other to be an appropriate "me" within the context of the best possible "us."

So how do you avoid flying off toward a remote part of the universe?

Talk to each other. Stay connected. Enjoy the warmth of both your internal passion and your partner's love.

My single New Year's resolution this year was that I would not allow myself to be terrified by criticism from Daveen. I am not saying that she is inherently critical, but only that I have allowed myself to be terrified. I have been reluctant to share some of my needs, afraid to be honest about a few of my actions, and scared by the possibility of her disapproval, real or imaginary. Please note that in making my New Year's resolution I have not asked Daveen to change anything about herself. My focus is on changing my reaction. Daveen is welcome to continue to be who she is, the person I have loved for almost thirty-five years, and respond to me as she will. It is my reaction that I desired to change, so that I could better stay connected with her.

As I continued my contemplation during the concert, I conjured the question: How do you maintain the heat of your passion—to be certain neither star cools into a lonely and frigid rock?

Remember that you are a separate star and can shine all by yourself. Last Sunday morning Daveen and I resurrected an old disagreement about something I am sensitive about. Normally I respond defensively and try to explain myself. But persuading Daveen to change her view on an issue she feels strongly about is a fool's errand. So my backup strategy has been to withdraw, quickly cooling from room temperature to absolute zero.

But this time I tried something different. "Daveen, in forty minutes I'm leaving for the studio to record the final section of my audiobook. I want to be in a good mood. I'm not going to engage in a discussion now that I know will upset us both." I wasn't angry. I did not withdraw, though I may have cooled a bit.

Daveen said, "Okay. Absolutely."

Daveen accompanied me and was helpful at the sound studio. We enjoyed a celebratory lunch together afterward. The heat of our mutual passion and respect remained, as it generally does, notwithstanding our occasional disagreements. As I recall, the potential argument disappeared into the heavens.

Any strong relationship must be mutually rewarding, which means that both partners must be stars that shine approximately equally most of the time.

If not, the two stars might fuse. Or they might find themselves in two separate cold and lonely parts of the universe.

You and your partner are the nearest stars to each other in the entire universe. Remaining in orbit around each other is what a mutual and supportive relationship is, the heart of two "me's" becoming an enduring "us."

THE SPOTLIGHT OF NOW

Whatever IS, is RIGHT.

—ALEXANDER POPE
An Essay on Man, Epistle 1

I accept the universe.

—MARGARET FULLER

Remark to Henry James, Sr., quoted in William James,
The Varieties of the Religious Experience

The auditorium of our future is always pitch-black, and we never know for sure what will happen in the time to come. We can write appointments on our calendars, pay in advance for our front row seat, and anticipate the appearance of a favorite guest. But even though we are always seated in the front row center of our lives, we can observe only the performance that the spotlight of "now" illuminates in a bright circle on stage.

I recently celebrated my seventy-fifth birthday at a dinner party on the top floor of a local hotel. Food was ordered, several hundred guests had been invited, and decorations were in place. A program was printed with the details of exactly what I expected to happen from 6:30 p.m. through the end of the evening.

But the spotlight of "now" did not shine on the prearranged program. I arrived half an hour late to my own party and missed most of the appetizers as well as a personalized balloon hat. I had the opportunity before dinner to greet only a few of many guests. Dinner was scheduled for 7:15, but everyone was talking and paying no attention to repeated requests to be seated.

Everything ran late. The magician cut his act short. The pianist never did have a moment to perform. When the wind quintet finished (late) my party planner rushed over to me and said, "I've lost control of the party."

I said, "No problem. Everyone seems to be enjoying themselves."

Since I was constantly surrounded by my more outgoing friends, many guests never pushed through the crowd to say "hello."

In short, everyone had a wonderful time.

It is said that life is what happens while you are busy making other plans. Hardly a day in my life has gone by without the spotlight of "now" shining on something I did not either plan or expect, proving time and again that I am not entirely in charge of my own life. I am, however, in charge of my reaction.

I have two rules for how to respond to the unexpected.

First, I ask myself if I can change my "now" back to what I expected, or to what I planned, at an acceptable cost. I'm sure I could have regained "control" of the party. I could have taken a microphone and loudly announced, "Okay, enough conversation. Please sit down for dinner because we're running late."

I think the cost of saying this, and putting the party back "on time," would have been to dampen the high spirits and reduce the energy in the room. I thought this cost was too high, so I made no announcement. I accepted the spotlight of "now," which was on the conversation, and not on the salad.

My second rule is that if I choose to allow the spotlight of "now" to shine where it will, I will simply smile, relax, and enjoy the journey. My objective for the party was to provide an environment in which my guests and I could have fun and create warm memories. That seemed to happen. But whether or not a plan succeeds, my job in living my life is to squeeze as much joy as possible out of every minute, which means to find the positive in whatever the spotlight of "now" reveals.

As I have written before, when I was fourteen I was a hospital patient for the first time, about to have my appendix removed. I was in serious pain and knew that my recovery from the operation would hurt even more. I reframed my situation, and thought, "This is great. This is going to really hurt, and for the rest of my life I will remember this day and always appreciate the absence of physical pain."

Your life, and every one of your relationships, will bring surprises. Not all will be happy. In spite of this, you are free to define whatever appears in your spotlight of "now" as positive. Your "me," your "us," and your "now" will be the better for it.

PEOPLE TOOL
FOR LOVE & RELATIONSHIPS
49

MAKE THE MOST OF TODAY

What will survive of us is love.
—PHILLIP LARKIN
"An Arundel Tomb," *The Whitsun Weddings*

*And in the end the love you take is
equal to the love you make.*
—JOHN LENNON AND PAUL MCCARTNEY
"The End" (song)

One day your relationship as a couple will end. This is not good news or bad news. It is a statement of a fact that each of us knows is certain. Our lives, and our relationships, will end. That is an inherent part of being human. The question is what will we do with the limited time we have?

My mantra in life is this. You only have today. Make the most of it.

Last Tuesday I spent the day with Melissa, a friend and business associate of many years. She almost canceled our meeting because her husband had just undergone a biopsy, and they were waiting to hear if he had a potentially terminal form of cancer. Ultimately, Melissa and her husband chose to go about their normal lives on Tuesday, even though both were justifiably concerned about his possible imminent death. They made the most of the day.

It's difficult to always remember that we have limited, precious time on Earth. When we are in the thick, or thin, of our lives—raising children, making love, earning money, worrying about personal or global catastrophes, real or imagined—we often forget for the moment how finite our lives really are, that we have been given only the idea of eternity and not eternity itself. I forget that myself. When I'm caught up in the busy-ness of the here and now, I forget all those unknowable future nows, from which I will soon enough be excluded.

When I am walking on a beach at sunset, hand in hand with my wife of almost thirty-five years, enjoying the fading of the light and my fantasy of what the evening may bring, why should I reflect, for even a moment, that it will not always be thus? That one day her hand will not be in mine, or mine in hers, or that this very evening may bring, for me, the beginning of eternal silence?

The purpose of my reflection is not to bring sadness into your life. It is to help me, and you, focus on the idea that we need to make the most of today—of this very moment.

When I was growing up, my parents were best friends with another couple, Marion and Irving. Irving earned his living in the dry cleaning business and Marion taught piano lessons. All the while they cherished their dream of taking a two-week vacation in Europe. They dreamed of climbing the Eiffel Tower, enjoying a fine meal at a French restaurant, and walking hand in hand along the Seine. This was in an era before jet planes made international travel more afford-able and this dream was almost beyond their reach. So they planned to take their trip of a lifetime as soon as Irving turned sixty-five and retired.

At age fifty-eight Irving suffered a massive heart attack and died within ten minutes.

Why did I remember and retell this story? My purpose, as I said, is not to immerse you, or myself, in a cloud of sorrow. Rather it is to remind each of us that our lives could end at any time and that this moment—here and now—is the only one we really have.

The whole idea of *People Tools for Love and Relationships: The Journey from Me to Us* is to help you do exactly that—squeeze the most out of each moment.

By "relationship" I am not referring exclusively to your primary relationship—your spouse or partner. To me two people who encounter each other in a transitory setting can have a relationship as well, even if only for a moment. This could be in the checkout line at the grocery store, or a conversation with a stranger on a park bench. It can also, of course, be with the partner with whom you have chosen to spend your life.

There is a thought I have carried with me for many years, "Experience is the best teacher. Preferably someone else's experience." I hope that you will allow my experience to help you make the most of every moment, and every relationship in your life. It is our relationships that, I believe, ultimately give our lives both their value and their meaning.

I hope that you will walk along that beach at sunset, or hand in hand beside the Seine, or even pace a hospital corridor, with fond memories of your past, deep immersion in your present, and soaring hope for your future.

And I hope that your experience of reading of this book will help you in your ongoing journey from "me" to "us," which, after all, is the most challenging and important journey of our lives.

LOVE IS THE ANSWER

There is only one happiness in life, to love and be loved.
—GEORGE SAND
Letter to Lina Calamatta, March, 31, 1862

All you need is love.
—SONG BY JOHN LENNON AND PAUL MCCARTNEY

This is the story of Jill, a seventy-year-old woman who lives by herself in a rented mobile home in a forest in Harbor, Oregon. Jill and I lived together for three years more than forty years ago. She is a four-foot-eleven-inch pixie with an infectious laugh and wild grey hair. Jill is generous and kind, and yet, like many of us, has led a life filled with obstacles.

When Jill was sixty-seven she underwent complex and painful spinal surgery. Her back problem was likely caused by the fact that she physically helped so many people for so many years that her back finally gave out. Just before her surgery Jill's husband of twenty years abandoned her. Even while they were together she realized he had been a man who welcomed care from her, but was not a care giver himself. Jill was left to recover from the operation at her daughter's home in San Diego.

After a year of frequent visits to her surgeon, bus trips for rehabilitation, and helping out her daughter as best she could by looking after her young granddaughter, Jill felt more and more like a stranger in a strange land.

"I have to leave," she told me. "I love my daughter and her husband and my granddaughter. They've been very nice to me, but I wasn't made for city life. I need to leave. I need to get back to the woods where I used to live."

Good health is the most important part of any life, and the place where you live may greatly contribute to, or detract from, your mental and physical well-being. For Jill it was important to inhale the forest perfume in the morning and to relax on her porch appreciating a sliver of the Pacific Ocean at dusk.

A few months later Jill did move back to Oregon, and to her freedom. "I just want to rent a little place outside of town. In the trees."

Like most of us, Jill had limited financial resources. But a few weeks after she returned to Oregon, Jill called.

"I found this cute little home less than a mile out of town, and I rented it. Thank you so much for all of your encouragement and support."

"That's great, Jill. As soon as we can, Daveen and I would love to come up for a visit."

People have always gone out of their way to be kind to Jill because she has always cheerfully taken care of them. I was delighted she had followed her dream.

On July 5th Jill called me.

"I'm so excited," she said. "Last night they had a fireworks show on the beach. I couldn't go because of my back, but I could see the beautiful colors through the trees. I sat on my front porch and I could see the fireworks. They were beautiful."

We are never too old or too weary to enjoy the simple pleasures of life. Fireworks on July 4th are one of those treats, as far as I am concerned.

Several months later Jill mentioned to me she that was helping others with part of the money I had sent to help her out. "Alan, I hope you don't mind, but I have a friend who's seventy-three. She needed a new walker, so I used some of the money to buy her one."

I was delighted that Jill was still helping others. "Of course it's okay. You can use that money any way you like." One or two months later Jill mentioned that she was also donating to the local food bank.

Today Jill's back has deteriorated further, and she is now housebound. She is unable even to take a taxi to town to shop for groceries. Her back can no longer tolerate the short journey, even though all of the cabbies in Harbor are now her friends and drove slowly and very carefully when Jill was their passenger. Fortunately Jill's doctor makes a house call whenever she needs him.

Last month Daveen, my one-hundred-year-old father, and I flew with Jill's daughter, son-in-law, and nine-year-old granddaughter to Crescent City, California. We rented a van for the drive to Harbor. We bought lunch and a few gifts at a local supermarket, and arrived at Jill's home a little after noon.

What a glorious day! This was the first time Jill's family had been able to visit in her new home. I watched her granddaughter rush around to take in the sights, with a delight allotted only to the young. I participated as everyone engaged with each other, revealing a deep sense of caring and connection.

"Alan, this is so great. I haven't seen your dad in what? Forty years?" Jill said.

A neighbor stopped by to be sure Jill was all right. I enjoyed a chat with Jill's son-in-law, who seemed dedicated to his profession and intent on climbing the slippery career ladder to success.

At day's end all of us gathered under the trees with many smiles and hugs goodbye, reluctant to let our joyful day with each other come to a close.

On our flight home I said to Daveen, "This has been one of the best days of my life."

Whatever the question, love is the answer. And at the end of our days, love is the best part of our lives, the part that really matters. To love and to be loved is truly the golden key to happiness.

© Alan Weissman Photography

Alan C. Fox has enjoyed a rich and varied professional life over during his seventy-five years. He has earned university degrees in Accounting, Law, Counseling, and Professional Writing. Alan was employed as a tax supervisor for a national CPA firm, before establishing his own law firm. He then founded a commercial real estate company in 1968 that today owns and manages many major income-producing properties in eleven states.

Alan is also the founder, editor, and publisher of *Rattle*, one of the most respected literary magazines in the United States, and sits on the board of directors of several non-profit foundations.

Alan's first book, *People Tools: 54 Strategies for Building Relationships, Creating Joy, and Embracing Prosperity*, was published in 2014 and was soon followed by *People Tools for Business: 50 Strategies for Building Success, Creating Wealth, and Finding Happiness*.

Alan now shares in *People Tools for Love and Relationships* what he has learned from his many years of experience in close relationships, including three marriages and raising six children, two step-children, one foster child, as well as many friendships and business relationships.

Subscribe to the weekly blog for inspiration and insight as Alan shares each Tuesday additional People Tools, stories, and more at peopletoolsbook.com.

Or contact Alan directly at alan@peopletoolsbook.com

 Facebook: PeopleToolsBook

 Twitter: @AlanCFox

 Instagram: @peopletools